Stop Overthinking

The Ultimate Guide to Eliminate Negative Thinking, Live in the Present Moment, and Achieve Emotional Wellness

Free Bonus from Andy Gardner

Hi!

My name is Andy Gardner, and first off, I want to THANK YOU for reading my book.

Now you have a chance to join my exclusive email list related to human psychology and self-development so you can get the ebook below for free as well as the potential to get more ebooks for free! Simply click the link below to join.

P.S. Remember that it's 100% free to join the list.

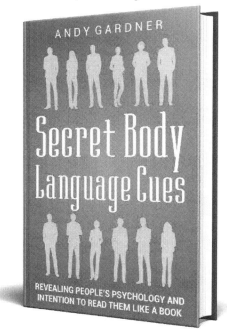

Access your free bonuses here:
https://livetolearn.lpages.co/andy-gardner-stop-overthinking-paperback/

Table of Contents

Introduction

People like to assume that they suffer setbacks and are incapable of going beyond certain hurdles in life because of external forces. They search all around for reasons or for people to blame for their failures. While this may be the case, they are usually wrong in one aspect. The enemy is not external; it is *internal.*

The force behind your failures is usually yourself – that small voice in your head that tells you that your next project will fail. This is a cross that every human bears, and those thought processes are powerful enough to hinder your progress. For some people, that voice is louder and more convincing than it is for others, which leads them to overthink.

Overthinking is not necessarily a bad thing. In fact, in some situations, it can be a huge advantage. However, it can also be a *huge burden* when you're trying to make an important decision.

In that situation, you begin to consider the voice in your head as an ally that wants to protect you from risk. It is at that point that the voice will advise you to abandon those "impossible" ideas.

If you are to be true to yourself, you will agree that overthinking things has actually hindered your ability to accomplish your goals more than it has helped you. There are things you may have passed up on because you thought they would make you look pathetic or chances you ignored because you weren't confident enough in professional or social situations.

Maybe you lost the motivation to try because you kept listening to and believing the self-deprecating and insecure voice telling you you're not good enough. You must understand that your inner limiting voice and your voice of reason are very different – don't confuse the two.

Millions of people in the world today feel trapped in the vicious cycle of negative thoughts that go in and out of their heads daily. Many of them complain that overthinking makes them indecisive and full of anxiety. So, if this is how you usually feel, know *you're not alone.*

If you want to break free from overthinking, or if you want to lead a life that is both fulfilling and positive, then you have come to the right place. This book is the perfect solution for those who are trapped in overthinking.

This book is exceptional because it emphasizes practical and easy-to-learn strategies _anyone_ can implement. It explains the psychology behind worries and overthinking while offering practical methods to help you recognize and overcome them.

"Stop Overthinking" is a must-read if you want to enhance your emotional and mental well-being. It doesn't matter if you have mild anxiety or severe symptoms. You will find a roadmap that can help you overcome your negative thought patterns and achieve greater happiness and peace in your daily life.

Starting today, read and implement this book's strategies and control your thoughts and emotions to live a more fulfilled life.

Chapter 1: Why We Overthink (Or The Psychology Behind Worrying)

William had a business meeting in New York the next week. He had bought his tickets, packed his bags, and prepared everything for the trip. However, he hadn't been able to sleep for three days. Many thoughts were rushing through his head. "What if I miss my flight?" "What if I arrive late to the meeting?" "What if I mess things up during the meeting?" "What if the plane crashes?" William struggled with these thoughts for a few days. He even missed his best friend's birthday because he was so engaged in his own world – stressed and drained.

When the day of the meeting came, he managed to catch the plane, arrive on time, and everything went better than he could ever have imagined. He had wasted his time and energy coming up with worst-case scenarios and creating a problem out of nothing.

One could argue that William's worrying helped him prepare for the meeting. However, he had no reason to worry since there wasn't an issue to begin with. They were all thoughts in his head – problems his *mind created.* He was obsessing over things out of his control and making up scenarios that were neither helpful nor rational.

Overthinking can cause you to become consumed with your thoughts.

Why was William's reaction to this situation to overthink? Why do people worry about things that are out of their control? What is the psychology behind these negative thoughts? This chapter answers all your questions, explaining why many people often get caught in these downward spirals of incessant thoughts.

Overthinking

Overthinking is the process of repetitively dwelling on the same thought, topic, or situation and analyzing every little detail to the point that you become consumed with these thoughts and unable to focus on any other area of your life. In other words, thinking too much about something and staying in a loop disrupts your life.

Psychologist Dr. Jeffrey Huttman defines overthinking as constantly analyzing your thoughts and emotions and fixating on past mistakes and decisions. American therapist Jessica Foley explains that overthinking is associated with unproductive thoughts like obsessing over past events and letting these thoughts impact your work or relationships.

Some people believe that overthinking isn't necessarily a bad thing or a character flaw since it helps them look at the problem from different angles, enabling them to arrive at the best solution and be prepared in case something unexpected happens. However, this isn't true.

Problem-solving is looking for answers to the questions you have been pondering, hoping to find a solution, while *overthinking* is dwelling or even obsessing about the pitfalls and possibilities of an issue with no real or effective results. These thoughts are usually only in your head, and the "problem" isn't even real.

Others confuse overthinking with self-reflection, but the two couldn't be more different. Self-reflection is characterized as a mental process where you contemplate questions about yourself to find your life's purpose and achieve personal growth. This is unlike negative thinking, where you obsess over your flaws with no intention of changing or growing.

Overthinking on occasion is normal. For instance, if you find out that your company is laying people off, you will naturally worry about whether you will be let go and how you will find a new job. In this case, the issue is real and present and requires your attention. Or, if you have a big presentation that could make or break your career, it is normal to worry and even imagine all the possible worst-case scenarios. This can motivate you to work hard and be prepared for all possible outcomes. Overthinking can be helpful when it doesn't take over your life and pushes you to take action and change things.

Over-thinkers don't just obsess over their problems; they also try to find meaning and purpose behind their thoughts. This can also be another advantage to overthinking. For instance, if you keep thinking about quitting your job or leaving your spouse, it will be helpful to analyze these thoughts, understand their causes, and what triggers them.

However, when overthinking interferes with your mental health and well-being, and you get lost in this unhealthy pattern to the point that every aspect of your life suffers, including your health, you have a problem. More often than not, these thoughts can be negative, and overanalyzing them can lead to obsession, guilt, anxiety, and depression.

However, overthinking is a character flaw but isn't part of who you are. In other words, it doesn't define you, and like any personality trait, it can be changed with the proper strategies.

The Psychology Behind Overthinking

Although overthinking isn't classified as a mental disorder, it is often associated with various mental disorders like post-traumatic stress disorder (PTSD), anxiety, and depression.

According to a 2015 study conducted by psychologist Bonnie N. Kaiser, overthinking can be caused by distress, and some cultures attribute mental illness to it, while others consider it to be a symptom of a mental disorder.

When you overthink, your thoughts trigger certain emotions. There is a thin line between anger/fear/excitement/loneliness/joy and overthinking and self-destruction. One simple thought like "Will I get laid off?" can take you on an endless road of negative thoughts and emotions like "What if I can't find another job?" or "I won't be able to pay the rent and my family will end up on the street."

Over-thinkers are often afraid of the future and are more focused on what could happen than what is already happening around them. This leads to anxiety and even depression.

According to neuropsychologist Sanam Hafeez, people overthink in an attempt to control a certain situation, as they believe this prepares them for what needs to be done. When you are worried or anxious, your brain resorts to overthinking to reduce your anxiety and make you feel better. You go through all the different outcomes to predict what will happen.

However, your brain gets stuck in this pattern of thought and can't get out of it to take the necessary actions. Even when you come up with a solution, your mind will raise more what-if questions, and you will find yourself in a loop; you can't find a solution or stop overthinking.

Researchers at the University of British Columbia noticed that certain personality types, like perfectionists, are more prone to overthinking. Dr. Hafeez also mentioned that perfectionists and overachievers usually overthink more than most people due to their fear of failure and desire to find the perfect 0utcome for every problem. As a result, they replay every situation in their heads and criticize every mistake and decision they make. They never seem to be able to find a solution because nothing is good enough – and they are only satisfied with perfection.

Dr. Huttman supports Dr. Hafeez's theory that only Type A personalities – which include intense, ambitious, and competitive individuals – are more likely to overthink than Type B personalities, who tend to be reactive, more relaxed, and less frantic.

Overthinking can be overwhelming, making you feel frustrated with constantly questioning all your feelings and decisions. You can't fight this urge to analyze every thought you have, especially random ones that often creep into your head. An over-thinker is often stuck in a cycle of anxiety of over-analysis.

Reasons People Overthink

Anxiety and worrying can lead to overthinking, but other things can drive you to obsess over your thoughts.

Worrying about the Future

Worrying about the future or an upcoming event can lead to overthinking. When you don't know what will happen, you try to develop your own version of how the events will unfold.

Trauma

Trauma often leads to overthinking. Certain traumatic events in your life can leave you vulnerable to obsess over every little detail and thought. Overthinking becomes a learned behavior that develops in childhood to deal with difficult situations.

For instance, if your parents were abusive and you lived your life always worrying, not knowing when they would come home drunk and lash out at you, you probably grew up into someone who is hyper-vigilant and who is always on high alert so you can quickly respond. This leads to obsessive thoughts and being constantly on edge.

Uncertainty

It is human nature to want to find out how every situation will turn out, especially where you have so much on the line, like your career or your relationship. Most people don't want to live with uncertainty, so they live in denial instead of convincing themselves that they can predict the outcome of any situation by overthinking. Overthinking gives them the false sense that they will eventually find a solution to the problem. Nothing in life is guaranteed, and no matter how hard you think, finding the answers you seek can be impossible.

Control

No one wants to feel helpless. It can even be harder when someone you care about is in a tough situation, and you don't know what to do for them. In some situations, you can help a loved one. A friend may need money, and you can afford to lend it to them. However, if a loved one has a serious disease or is dying, there is nothing more you can do other than offer your love and support. It can be hard for some people to face their own limitations and accept their helplessness, so they resort to overthinking.

These thoughts are useless, but they make you feel like you are doing something to help. In other words, these thoughts give you a false sense of control and make you feel useful. However, this habit can damage your mental health and cause stress, low self-esteem, and chronic anxiety. Once you make peace with the fact that you can't possibly control every aspect of your or other people's lives, you will rely less on overthinking.

Perfectionism

Perfectionists don't want to be perfect; they want to feel perfect. Whether it is their work, clothes, car, appearance, or any other part of their life, they often obsess over it until they feel it's immaculate. For instance, you prepared a presentation you will show your boss tomorrow. However, you cannot sleep because you feel that your work isn't perfect. You keep thinking about what you can do or add to your presentation so it is flawless. Subconsciously, you find these thoughts helpful since they distract you from the fact that your work isn't on the unrealistic level you want it to be. Perfectionism usually stems from the inability to tolerate inadequacy. Accepting that things can just be good enough is a great step to fighting overthinking.

Getting Something Out of It

Sometimes people overthink because they get something out of it. For instance, someone may obsess over a situation simply because it garners their sympathy, while others use overthinking as an excuse to put off making a decision or avoid it completely. Or, if they make a bad decision, they can tell themselves that they just didn't have enough time to think about it.

It is important to understand why you resort to this tactic and what you really get out of it, as only then will you be able to grow and change.

Avoiding Conflict

Most people don't enjoy conflict and prefer to avoid it at all costs. As a result, they don't have no experience handling confrontations and struggle during these situations. This leads to irrational avoidance and fear of conflict. You find yourself always thinking of ways to avoid conflict in every intense situation, leading to overthinking. In fact, learning how to handle conflict is a lot easier than worrying about preventing every interaction from turning into an argument.

Overgeneralization

If overthinking one area of your life has helped you, you believe it will benefit you in all other aspects. Although it can be positive in some situations, that doesn't guarantee that it will bring you the same results in others. Imagine overthinking as a tool and your house representing your entire life. Would you use the same tool to fix every broken part in your home? Of course not.

You have to separate the areas in your life where overthinking is effective from the ones where it is utterly useless.

Types of Overthinking

Everyone has their own reason for overthinking, but it is usually connected to cognitive distortion. This can be defined as a negative pattern of thinking that is usually irrational and can cause low self-esteem, stress, anxiety, and depression.

Catastrophizing

Catastrophizing is imaging the worst-case scenario in every situation. For instance, you have a job interview, and you keep thinking that you will not get the job because there are other candidates better than you, and the interviewer won't like you and may even laugh at you. This will eventually get to you, lower your self-esteem, and you will fail to get the job.

All or Nothing

When one sees everything in life as either black or white – that's an unrealistic way of thinking. You may be only looking at a situation from one side – that is, you will either succeed and have it all OR fail and end up with nothing.

Jumping to Conclusions

Over-thinkers believe they can read people's minds and know what they think or how they will react. They also believe they can predict the future and the outcome of every situation. Over-thinkers jump to these conclusions based on their distorted thinking pattern, meaning they never consider the facts, leading them to make untrue speculations.

Rumination

Rumination is obsessing over the past and replaying different scenarios in your head. You may think of how you could have done things differently or worry about an upcoming event. Since the past is already gone and you have no control over the future, these thoughts are often futile and exhausting. You aren't overthinking to improve things; you are only worrying yourself for no reason. You usually experience these thoughts when you are nervous, scared, or anxious about an upcoming event like a job interview or an exam. Instead of preparing yourself, you entertain your anxiety with negative thoughts that will only make you feel worse.

You may also think of all the times you messed up in a job interview or failed an exam which will impact your self-esteem and ruin your chances of actually getting the job or passing the test.

Worrying and Anxiety

Worrying is feeling concerned or uneasy about a problem, event, or situation. You can worry about your relationship, career, money, health, or any other aspect of your life. Unlike overthinking, worrying is more realistic and based on real concerns rather than thoughts in your head. It usually results from stress and motivates you to take action and solve the problem.

However, like anything, worrying has a negative side. It can usually exaggerate the situation, and you find yourself coming up with negative possibilities. Once one negative thought creeps in, others quickly follow it, making you feel overwhelmed and stressed. In fact, you will not only imagine the worst-case scenario but also believe it has already happened. For instance, a mother keeps calling her teenage son, but he isn't answering his phone. He was supposed to return home at 10 pm, but now it is midnight, and he hasn't returned yet. She becomes so worried that she believes he has had a terrible accident. According to Psychology Today, the human brain sometimes fails to distinguish between reality and imagination. In this situation, her mind can't tell the difference between her concerns and what is really happening, so worrying turns into rumination.

On the other hand, anxiety is perceiving a situation as dangerous and extremely stressful. Unlike both worrying and overthinking, anxiety is a mental disorder. It lasts longer than worrying, can trigger a physical reaction like shaking or difficulty breathing, isn't often based on a real concern as it depends on your perception of the situation, can interfere with your daily life, and is hard to manage.

Some people use *worry* and *anxiety* interchangeably, but the two words are very different. This example will clarify how they differ from each other.

Worry

Jessica is afraid of heights, and whenever she visits her sister, who lives on the fifteenth floor, and she sees her window, she feels worried and stressed. The worrying prompts her to sit away from the window, and she feels better and more relaxed when she does that.

Anxiety

Jessica is so afraid of heights that even tall buildings make her nervous. Her fear is always on her mind, and whenever she is on a high floor, she gets a panic attack, and her heart beats fast. This feeling stays with her for long periods and impacts every aspect of her life.

Disclaimer: This book will provide helpful tools to combat overthinking but mental disorders like anxiety require the help of a professional.

How Do Worrying and Rumination Work?

In your temporal lobe, there is a part called the amygdala. It sends an alert signal to the prefrontal cortex to analyze the worry you are experiencing. However, it doesn't come up with a solution or try to ease concerns. The prefrontal cortex comes up with all the negative outcomes of the situation, creating a "feedback loop." This is a vicious cycle of magnifying every concern you have between the amygdala and the prefrontal cortex.

To simplify things, imagine you tell your friend that your partner has been distant lately, and you are worried they may have problems at work they aren't telling you about. However, your friend tells you that things could be worse and that your partner may be cheating on you and is probably distant because they want to leave you. In this situation, you are the amygdala, and your friend is the prefrontal cortex turning a simple concern into something much worse.

Negative Thinking

Negative thinking ignores the positive aspect of any situation and only focuses on the negative. This thought pattern is usually illogical because it dismisses rational thinking and only focuses on what can go wrong. For instance, someone with one bad relationship believes they are destined to be alone and will never meet a decent person.

Negative thinking usually magnifies the negative and minimizes the positive. Using the previous example, the person is only focused on this one bad relationship and ignores all the times they were happy and in love.

Can You Stop Overthinking?

Yes, you can. You can eliminate this personality flaw with the proper tools and strategies by understanding the reasons behind it and what triggers it. This book contains effective exercises and advice that you can implement to combat and get rid of overthinking once and for all.

Disclaimer: If overthinking is a symptom of mental illness, you will require the help of a professional.

Are You an Over-thinker?

Take this quiz and find out if you are an over-thinker.

1. Can you control your thoughts?
    - Yes
    - No
2. Do negative thoughts often creep into your head?
    - Yes
    - No
3. Do you believe you must be in control of your thoughts?
    - Yes
    - No
4. Are you curious about how your mind functions?
    - Yes
    - No
5. Do you usually focus on your thoughts when you are upset?
    - Yes
    - No

6. Are you often curious about the meaning or purpose behind your thoughts?

- Yes
- No

7. Do you often wonder why you experience these negative or persistent thoughts?

- Yes
- No

8. Are you always aware of your thoughts?

- Yes
- No

9. Do you get so focused on one problem that you are unable to think about anything else?

- Yes
- No

10. Do you keep thinking about a problem even when you find a solution?

- Yes
- No

11. Do your thoughts put you in a bad mood?

- Yes
- No

12. Do you usually find yourself obsessing over the past or worried about the future?

- Yes
- No

13. Do you keep replaying past situations in your mind?

- Yes
- No

14. Do you often think of the worst-case scenario in any situation?

- Yes
- No

15. Do you repeatedly think about the same worries or fears?
- Yes
- No

16. Does your mind race with so many thoughts that you cannot relax?
- Yes
- No

17. Are you always worried or anxious?
- Yes
- No

18. Do you often fixate on things that are out of your control?
- Yes
- No

19. Do you second-guess every decision you make?
- Yes
- No

20. Do you believe you are an over-thinker?
- Yes
- No

You are an over-thinker if you answer with "Yes" to most of these questions. Don't worry, though. You aren't alone. Many people tend to think too much. However, for every problem, there is a solution, and since you have already decided to change, you are on the right track.

Overthinking can lower the quality of your life. You can become so consumed with your negative thoughts and forget to live, enjoy yourself, or see all the good things around you. You are always exhausted since your brain never shuts down but keeps coming up with scenarios with no purpose other than stressing you.

You have the power to change your life. Understanding the psychology behind overthinking demonstrates that there is a root cause to these thoughts. Once you figure out whether your need for perfection or your childhood trauma makes you adopt this thought pattern, you can take the necessary steps to change.

Chapter 2: Observing Thoughts and Emotions

If you feel like you have too many negative thoughts and emotions, regardless of what's happening in your life, know you're not alone. Overthinking and obsessing about things that may or may not happen is a trait many people have. It is more common than you may imagine. Almost everyone has to deal with the overwhelming and exhausting emotions that come with negative thinking sometimes. Some days, you may wake up with a heart full of dread, anxiety churning in your stomach, and an overwhelming sense of sadness. Even if you try to shake this never-ending sadness off, it lingers throughout the day, often draining your energy and affecting how you interact with others. It may even feel like you're carrying an invisible boulder you can't seem to put down.

Overthinking can cause a multitude of negative emotions.
https://unsplash.com/photos/GVDV9tKGars?utm_source=unsplash&utm_medium=referral&utm_content=creditShareLink

This kind of emotional behavior is very common in people plagued with negative thoughts and emotions. However, there's always a way to deal with its negative effects on your mental state. The first step is to learn how to observe your emotions and thoughts. When you identify and classify what you're feeling, you'll be able to manage your emotions much more effectively. This chapter is all about helping you do that. Once you observe and identify your thoughts and feelings, you'll gain a much deeper understanding of what triggers your negative thought patterns. This chapter will also include some practical strategies that will help you build resilience toward the negative thoughts and feelings that arise whenever you face your triggers.

Remember, dealing with negative emotions can be very tough. However, shying away from or hiding from these emotions isn't healthy either. You shouldn't, under any circumstances, ignore or suppress your negative emotions because they will ultimately resurface again. You should acknowledge and accept these emotions and develop healthy management techniques. As the quote by psychologist Carl Jung goes, "What you resist, persists." Think of your negative feelings like a bouncy ball you're trying to push underwater; no matter how hard you push, it will always float back up due to the water pressure.

Similarly, pushing your feelings deeper inside will never help you eliminate them and will only worsen them. So, take the first step toward breaking free from your cycle of rumination, self-doubt, and negative thoughts by identifying how you're feeling. It won't be easy, but with steadfast determination, you'll achieve your goals in no time.

Understanding Emotions

Do you ever think about what your emotions really are? Are they simply fleeting sensations that come and go, or are they more than that? It's inarguable that emotions are complex and multifaceted, and they primarily exist to serve a variety of purposes. Think of emotions like the colors of your inner landscape, either your soul or personality. They're the hues that paint your mood and shape your perception of the world. If you think from a scientific perspective, emotions are energy in motion. Your brain uses your emotions to communicate with you. Depending on your emotional state, they can be subtle, overwhelming, intense, or fleeting. They can be pleasant or unpleasant, positive or negative, but regardless of their nature, emotions are there to provide you with valuable information about yourself.

Many people have the misconception that they should always act on their emotions right away. However, they aren't always rational. In fact, they're often misleading and irrational, which is why you should never act on them immediately. Instead, you should take some time to understand why you feel a particular emotion and then take action. Similar to how a canvas needs time to dry before you can add more paint, your emotions need space before you can act on them. They are a double-edged sword, though. If you repress or avoid them, they will likely fester and grow. The best way to deal with negative emotions is to first identify and acknowledge them.

To become more aware of your emotions, you must go through a journey of self-discovery and self-acceptance. You'll need to unravel the many layers of your emotional landscape and learn to embrace the colors that make you who you are. In this journey, you'll have to face your fears, confront your demons, and ultimately come out stronger on the other side. Just know that there's no escaping your emotions, and you'll have to feel them, if not now, then sometime eventually. So, it's better to not repress your emotions but instead deal with them in a healthy way.

Observing and Identifying Emotions

Observing your emotions may not be as easy as you think. It's definitely something many people struggle with. More often than not, people feel that their emotions are controlling them rather than being the other way around. This is especially true for people who struggle with overthinking habits and negative thought patterns. Suppose you're dealing with a serious mental health issue. In that case, observing and identifying your emotions will not be an effective long-term solution. In that case, in addition to using the techniques provided in this chapter, you should seek professional help.

When you understand how you're feeling, you can start to take control of your actions and even your emotions and respond to them in a healthy manner instead of lashing out or suppressing them. Doing this will allow you to break free of negative thought patterns and destructive coping mechanisms. But, as you know, observing and accepting your emotions isn't always easy. In the beginning, it'll seem very uncomfortable – and even painful – to confront your feelings. However, with time and practice, you'll develop the skills needed to manage them in a healthy manner. So, if you're struggling with negative emotions or overthinking issues, take some time to reflect on your emotional experiences. Identify the specific emotions you're dealing with and the corresponding triggers that have contributed to them. Here are some ways you can do that:

1. The Mental Check-In

One of the easiest techniques to identify exactly what you're feeling at a particular moment is the mental check-in. It is perfect for identifying any negative emotions you're feeling. It also helps you figure out what thoughts you're getting as a result of these emotions and how your behavior reflects your thoughts. It's basically a mental scan of your emotional state.

To understand how you can use this technique, consider the following example. Suppose you're at work, and you've just received some feedback from your supervisor. The feedback is more critical than you expected, and you start feeling your heart racing and a knot forming in your stomach. You may even notice negative thoughts running through your mind, like, "I'm not good enough," "Why do I always mess things up?" or "Why does everything bad happen to me?" This is when you should practice this technique to understand where these thoughts are coming from. Take a deep breath, and do a mental check-in with yourself by asking these questions:

- What am I feeling right now?
- Where am I feeling it in my body?
- What thoughts are running through my mind?

One by one, answer these questions, either by writing them down or simply in your head, and you'll notice that with each answer, you become more aware of what your current emotional state is like and what emotions you're feeling. In this case, you may feel angry, anxious, embarrassed, sad, or even hopeless. Here's a checklist of questions you can use to guide your mental check-in:

- **What am I feeling right now?**
  - Am I feeling anxious, angry, sad, or overwhelmed?
  - Am I feeling any physical sensations in my body, like tension, pain, or a racing heartbeat?

- On a scale of 1 to 10, how intense is the emotion I'm feeling?

- **Where am I feeling it in my body?**
  - Am I feeling any tension, discomfort, or pain in a specific area of my body?
  - Is there any particular sensation that's more noticeable than the rest?

- **What thoughts are running through my mind?**
  - Am I having any negative thoughts, like self-criticism, rumination, or catastrophic thinking?
  - Are these thoughts really helpful or not?
  - Can I challenge these thoughts with evidence or a different perspective?

2. Mindful Meditation

Another effective way to identify and observe your emotions is through mindfulness meditation practices. Mindfulness is basically the practice of being present and aware of your thoughts, emotions, and physical sensations in the present moment. You can use this technique whenever you feel overwhelmed by negative emotions and overthinking. For example, if you start to feel anxious before a big presentation, this technique is the solution. Once you identify what emotion you're feeling, you'll be able to deal with it easier and more manageable. To practice mindful meditation, get into a comfortable position, preferably somewhere you won't be disturbed. Take a few deep breaths and then follow these steps:

1. Starting from your head, try to notice all physical sensations you're feeling. Do you feel discomfort, tightness, or tension? Simply observe these sensations instead of acting on them. You may feel tightness in your chest or a knot in your stomach, your heartbeat may be beating much faster, or you could simply just have an unusually painful headache.

2. Once you've observed the physical sensations you're feeling, shift your attention to your breathing. Notice how your breath enters and exits your body. Empty your mind, and simply focus on how you breathe. If your breathing is fast, gradually slow it down until your heartbeat settles.

3. Keep focusing on your breath and shoot down any thoughts that pop up. Keep your attention on your breathing instead of getting caught up in whatever thoughts or emotions you're experiencing. Treat your emotions and thoughts as clouds passing by in the sky. Don't suppress or judge them. Instead, just acknowledge their presence and let them pass.

4. Once you've taken note of your emotions, separate them out, and label them. In this case, you may feel nervous, scared, or anxious, and labeling your thoughts will help you stay in control.

5. Remember that emotions are a normal part of being human, even if those emotions make you feel weak. Instead of beating yourself up about it, you should be compassionate and kind to yourself.

Practice this technique regularly to observe your emotions at any given moment. The more you practice, the better you'll get at observing and labeling what you're feeling.

3. Journaling

What's better than writing down your thoughts and exploring your emotions in a journal setting? This exercise is proven to help you gain control over your emotions, manage negative thought patterns, and identify triggers. Here are some journaling ideas you can incorporate into your routine:

a. **Freewriting**

Freewriting is exactly what it sounds like. Just write whatever comes to mind. It could be negative thoughts, doubts, or overthinking patterns. Simply set a timer for 10 to 15 minutes and let your pen flow. Don't worry about grammar, punctuation, or coherence; simply write your heart out! This will help you identify themes and patterns in your emotional state.

b. **Brainstorming Solutions**

If you're struggling with an overthinking issue that makes you question everything, use your journal to brainstorm solutions. Write down as many thoughts as possible, even if they seem silly, unrealistic, or irrational. Then, write down solutions to these problems. Also, consider if the problem is something you can control. If not, there's no need to dwell on it any longer.

c. **Stream of Consciousness**

This technique is similar to freewriting and involves writing down your thoughts as you think them but with a bit more structure. You can start with a journal prompt like, "What am I feeling right now?" or "What's in my mind today?" and let your thoughts flow. For instance, maybe you're feeling anxious, but you haven't been able to figure out why. Doing this exercise will allow you to identify why you're feeling anxious and review your thoughts when they arise.

d. **Emotion Mapping**

Emotion mapping in your journal will help you identify the behaviors and triggers associated with certain emotions. To do this, draw a circle in the middle of the page, and inside the circle, write down whatever emotion you're feeling. Once you've done that, draw a few lines from the circle, and at the end of each line, write down any triggers you can think of and the behavior that results in this emotion. For example, if you're feeling angry, write it down, along with the triggers for it AND the associated behavior (like clenched fists, racing thoughts, or yelling.)

e. **Dialogue Journaling**

Dialogue journaling is effective – and a fun way to use your creativity to express your emotions. For this exercise, write a conversation between yourself and the emotions you're experiencing. Ask questions, express how it's making you behave, and come up with responses from its side. This technique can help you better understand your emotions and work through any issues you may face. This is what dialogue journaling can look like:

Emotion: Anxiety

Journal Entry:

"Today, I'm feeling really anxious about an upcoming job interview. My mind is racing with thoughts of what could go wrong and how I may mess it up. I don't know how to calm down and get a grip on my nerves."

Dialogue Journaling:

→ *You: Hey, Anxiety. I see you're here again.*

→ *Anxiety: Yeah, I'm back. You have that interview coming up, remember?*

→ *You: Yeah, I do. But I'm feeling really nervous about it.*

→ *Anxiety: That's because you're worried about not getting the job. You're afraid you're not good enough.*

→ *You: Yeah, I guess that's true. But I've prepared for this interview and have some good experience.*

→ *Anxiety: But what if they don't like you? What if you mess up?*

→ *You: I know those thoughts are coming from you, Anxiety. But I'm going to try my best, and that's all I can do. I don't need to be perfect.*

→ *Anxiety: Okay, I hear you. But I'm still going to be here with you during the interview.*

→ *You: That's okay. I know you're just trying to protect me. I'm going to do my best to manage you and not let you take over.*

This technique pushes you to have a conversation with your emotions and better understand where they're coming from.

4. Worry List

This method is perfect for over-thinkers who find themselves struggling with anxiety-inducing and unrealistic thoughts. Writing down your thoughts can be a great way to put your mind at ease. Create a worry list where you write down all your thoughts and worries. Keep this list on hand throughout your day and add to it whenever you're dealing with more worries – no matter how big or small. Remember to not judge yourself when writing down your thoughts, and learn to practice self-compassion and treat yourself as you would treat a friend struggling with negative thoughts or self-doubts.

For example, maybe you notice you constantly worrying about your performance at work, even when you are not on the clock. By writing this down, you can identify this as a common source of worry and work toward developing coping strategies to manage it.

5. Thought Labeling

Another way to stop yourself from going down the rabbit hole of negative thoughts is by labeling the ones you have. You can either label them as positive, negative, or neutral. For instance, let's assume you're at home and suddenly start thinking about what happened at work earlier in the day. Maybe a colleague said something rude to you, or maybe your supervisor was too critical of your work. Instead of getting lost in the details of the situation, and reliving that event, try to label this thought as positive or negative. If you thought something like, "I can't believe they said that to me," this will count as a negative thought. Or, if you think, "I'm so grateful for my supportive colleagues for having my back today," this would be labeled as positive. Labeling your thoughts will allow you to identify your patterns and tell you whether you're prone to thinking negative thoughts or if positive thoughts are a part of your routine too. This will also help you challenge the negative thoughts you have and come up with ways to deal with said thoughts. You could also make a checklist with positive and negative labels, and whenever a thought pops up, pause and think of where it belongs.

6. Time Travel

Have you ever thought about an embarrassing moment and wished that you could travel back in time to change what you did? Sadly, time travel is not an option. However, there is a technique that can help you get a new perspective regarding the negative thoughts and feelings you're having. Whenever you're thinking of a particular situation that makes you have negative thoughts, take a few deep breaths and picture yourself looking down at that situation from a bird's eye view. Visualize yourself watching the scene play out. Observe the situation from afar and try to be as emotionally detached from it as possible. Think about what piece of advice you would give to a friend if this was their situation. When you take yourself out of the situation and view it from a different perspective, you'll be much less likely to have negative thoughts associated with it. In fact, you may even come up with new solutions for your problem.

Your thoughts are just in your brain. Why are you letting your thoughts have physical control over your whole body? Your thoughts don't define you, and you have the power to control them. With the techniques and exercises you've gone through in this chapter, you can take charge of your thoughts and start to live in the present moment instead of being in your head all the time. It won't be easy at first, but soon enough, you'll gain mastery over controlling your thoughts and emotions and develop healthy coping mechanisms.

Chapter 3: Questioning Your Story

In this chapter, you will learn how to assess and better understand the thoughts and beliefs that lead to stress, overthinking, and worry. You'll find out about unhealthy ways which may be determining your self-worth and learn how to challenge these thoughts. It also explains how you can change your negative self-beliefs into more constructive ones and provides tips on changing how you measure your self-worth.

Understand Your Narrative

Understanding your narrative can help you answer questions about yourself.
https://unsplash.com/photos/Oaqk7qqNh_c?utm_source=unsplash&utm_medium=referral&utm_content=creditShareLink

Most people struggle to answer simple questions about themselves. They're not entirely sure about who they truly are when they are alone. They don't know when or where they feel most at ease and can't pinpoint the situations that make them feel on edge. Some people don't know anything about their personal beliefs, thoughts, and values and have formulated inaccurate opinions about themselves over time.

You must understand your narrative to understand what makes you worry and keeps you awake at night. You must explore the stories you've made up about yourself and the world around you. You need to explore your perceptions and beliefs to find out what exactly makes you anxious.

The key here is not to question why you are the person you are but to understand and accept yourself as a whole. Self-awareness is essential for happiness. Understanding yourself lifts a lot of weight off your shoulders. It lets you let go of all the harmful beliefs you hold on to, identify your triggers, and build strong boundaries. This amount of self-understanding allows you to choose happiness and nourish your mind, soul, and body.

Take a moment to think about how you measure your self-worth. Do you tell yourself that you'll never be successful after a bad day at work? Do you feel bad the entire day if you notice your belly is bloated in the morning? Perhaps you tell yourself that no one will ever love you if you're not successful.

You may have never thought about how you measure your self-worth but may have noticed that your opinions about yourself can change multiple times a day. You'll never have a solid sense of self-worth – which is needed for mental and emotional health – if you ascribe your value to random factors like your wealth, appearance, or the number of friends you have. You'll feel over the moon when you meet the standards that you've set for yourself and experience a mental breakdown whenever you fall short.

There are several ways to determine your worth, many of which are detrimental. Here are a few of the most common and unhealthy ways people determine their value in life:

Appearance

If you feel insecure whenever the numbers on the scale go up, engage in self-deprecating talk because your jeans feel tighter than usual, feel bad on days no one compliments you, or feel worthy whenever someone notices your weight loss/weight gain efforts, then you likely measure your value using your appearance.

You are so much more than a face and a body. Bodies are just vessels through which souls experience life. Good looks can certainly make life a lot easier and put you at an advantage. However, being pretty can only get you so far.

Besides, bodies change drastically throughout your life – and looks fade over time. If you continue to tie your self-worth to your appearance, dealing with wrinkles, gray hair, or hair loss, which all come with aging, can feel like the end of the world.

If you ask people why they love their friends, they'll say that they love them because they're generous, kind, compassionate, loyal, helpful, caring, or fun. No one loves their friend just because they have the "perfect body" or pearly white teeth. People like to surround themselves with friends and family who are *good for their spirit.*

Unless they're shallow, your friends don't care how you look. If they do, then you probably don't want them in your life anyway. When you die, no one will say, "Oh, I miss them so much. They had a flat stomach and clear skin." They're going to remember the *impact* you had on their lives.

Net Worth

Some people tie their sense of worthiness to their material possessions and the amount of money they make. Suppose you grew up in a financially unstable household or in a community that defines success using wealth. In that case, you might feel that your success in life is measured by the size of your bank account or the car you drive, all of which therefore determine your worth.

This can cause you to believe that your financial status is the most important thing in life, blinding you from what really matters. Working a job that doesn't meet your definition of financial success or experiencing rough financial periods can make you feel worthless and inadequate. You may often fear checking your bank account or reviewing your finances.

Your income, car, watch, and designer clothes aren't rational ways to gain the approval and acceptance of society. Having good values and morals is what earns you the love and respect of your community. Your success should be defined by your own happiness and personal growth and development. If you're truly happy with who you are and everything you're doing, then you're already ahead of half the population. Success doesn't mean much when you're miserable.

You'll never feel good enough about yourself if you continue to base your self-esteem on your net worth. Regardless of how much money people make, they often search for ways to make more. Even the world's richest people are always searching for ways to increase their wealth, which is why using money to determine your success and worth will always leave you feeling inadequate.

Social Network

Many people base their self-worth on the people they know because they believe that their social circle reflects their achievements, personalities, wealth, prestige, and qualities. Everyone falls into the trap of comparing themselves to other people's social status and standing, and many societies associate a person's social circle with their worth and success.

Your reputation and social status can undeniably be affected by the people you spend your time with. As Jim Rohn once said, "*You are the average of the five people you spend the most time with.*" Your social circle can affect your behavior and attitude. Spend time with people you look up to because you want to learn from them and not because you want to name-drop and feel good about yourself.

Using your social network as a measure of your self-worth causes you to seek out connections that are not genuine, which can ruin your relationships over time. Your worth and purpose in life should be attributed to your contributions to the world and not the achievements of others.

Once you lose these connections, you'll feel lost and invaluable. Feeling worthy just because you associate with influential or important people is one of the most damaging things you can do to yourself. It causes you to lead a fake life, and when it all ends, you'll discover that you know nothing about yourself and didn't amount to anything in life. Strive to portray the qualities you admire about your social connections. Learn from them, but don't feel worthy just because you have them. You'll never receive everyone's admiration and respect, regardless of who your best friend or aunt is.

Career

Many societies judge the success and worth of individuals based on their career paths. For instance, in some Asian and Arab countries, some parents take pride in their kids studying to be doctors and engineers and shame those who let their children go to business or art school. Hustle culture also promotes the idea that success is tied to your career, productivity, and how much you work. If you grew up affected by similar mindsets, then you may link your self-worth to your professional life.

Your career might be the primary source of fulfillment, purpose, and identity. Receiving compliments from your boss or co-workers and getting promoted can improve your sense of self-worth and self-esteem. On the other hand, career-related problems can feel catastrophic.

Viewing your self-worth as a reflection of your career success can lead to burnout. You'll prioritize your job, blurring the lines between your personal and professional life. This will negatively impact your relationships, cause you to neglect self-care, and pull you away from your hobbies and other aspects that shape your identity.

You're limiting yourself by allowing your career to shape your worth. You'll feel the need to achieve to feel validated, which keeps you from improving other areas of your life and pursuing things that can make you feel more fulfilled. It can also make you miss out on other invaluable experiences that lead to personal growth and development.

Tomorrow isn't guaranteed. A global crisis like the coronavirus pandemic, a personal health issue, or an economic downturn can negatively affect your career or even put an end to it. Tying your self-worth to something as unstable as your job can destroy your sense of purpose and identity.

Achievements

Accomplishments make people feel recognized and validated. They offer hard proof that someone is talented, skilled, and hard-working, which would normally boost their self-esteem and sense of pride. Accomplishments are rewarded in nearly every setting in the world. Athletes receive medals, students earn certificates or scholarships, and employees get raises or promotions. Family members brag about each other's accomplishments, and everyone suddenly congratulates you and takes pride in knowing you when you excel in something. This is why many people feel most worthy when they accomplish things.

However, tying your self-worth to your accomplishments can make you feel pressured to achieve and be recognized for your work. It makes you want to prove yourself to the world, leading to substantial self-doubt when you experience setbacks. Suppose you initially loved what you do and felt happy and fulfilled doing it. In that case, your passion will become a source of pressure and stress once you set lofty expectations for yourself.

You could develop a fear of failure if you use your accomplishments to measure your self-worth. Over time, you'll realize that mistakes and difficulties take a major blow to your self-esteem. This keeps you stuck and prevents you from taking potentially fruitful risks and pursuing new opportunities. You'll never learn and grow if you stay in your comfort zone.

Your achievements don't just rely on your personal abilities and strengths. Often, your efforts can be disrupted due to external factors. The opinions of others, certain circumstances, and the performance of competing entities can change the dynamic. You won't always be the best at everything; if you don't accept this, you'll never stop struggling.

How to Change Your Negative Self Beliefs

Identify Your Thoughts and Feelings

Now that you have a better idea about how you measure your self-worth, it's time to identify your thought patterns. Whenever you feel bad about yourself or engage in negative self-talk, walk yourself through a series of self-inquiries. Give yourself a few minutes to calm down and focus on your feelings. Where do you feel the frustration, anxiety, or negative emotion in your body? Describe what it feels like and explore the accompanying thoughts.

Ask yourself if your thoughts and the statements you've made about yourself are true. Then, ask yourself where these thoughts came from. Do they result from your beliefs, or did someone else's words or actions influence them? Determine if your thoughts are based on solid facts or just emotions. Is there any evidence that could point to the accuracy of these thoughts? What evidence tells you that they're inaccurate? What can you do to test the validity of this thought? Think about why this belief makes you feel worried or anxious. What's the worst that could happen if the scenario you're worried about happened or your beliefs turned out to be true?

Whenever you make statements about yourself, dampen their impact by phrasing them as feelings. For instance, if you think you lack strength or resilience, change the statement from "I'm weak" to "I feel weak." Notice the change in impact and emphasis. This simple rephrase puts things into perspective.

Telling yourself that you're weak reinforces that negative idea. You're stating it like a fact, making it harder for yourself to counter. However, if you state it like a mere emotion, you'll recognize that this is just a feeling that doesn't necessarily carry much depth and truth. When you separate yourself from the description and recognize that you aren't that adjective, you can explore why you feel that way and understand what's behind your emotions.

Accept Your Feelings

Repeat these feelings to yourself without engaging with them. Don't judge or falsify them- just accept them as they are. Cry if you want to, feel the tension in your body, and breathe. Meditate on past situations when you felt like this and why you feel this way.

It's not easy to accept these feelings about yourself, but it's an important step if you want to achieve peace and release these emotions once and for all. You can't let go of something that you don't accept. The best you can do is suppress it, creating additional problems later on.

Generate New Truths

After you accept these beliefs, practice reframing your thoughts and turning them into more constructive ones. Back your new truth with evidence and logical thinking, and truly believe in what you're telling yourself.

For example, instead of "I feel weak," you can tell yourself, "I'm not weak. I'm only experiencing a rough period right now. I'm going through a breakup/ family problems/ work issues, etc., which can be a lot to deal with. I accept my feelings and believe I will come out of all this much stronger."

Acknowledging your feelings and the reasons behind them brings your attention to your strengths and qualities. You start actively searching for reasons why your negative beliefs aren't true.

Repeat Your New Belief

Repeat this new truth to yourself as often as you can. Treat it like an affirmation so your subconscious mind starts believing the words and adopting this truth. Notice the differences in the feelings that arise when you speak positively about yourself and when you hold negative beliefs. Ask yourself which thoughts make you feel better and which sound believable.

Your new beliefs are true because if you were truly weak, incapable, or unlovable, you would never have noticed a deficiency in these qualities and criticized yourself for them in the first place. They're just feelings that arise when you're going through a hard time.

You may feel a profound difference or nothing at all when you first start doing this. However, you'll start accepting and living by your new truth over time. It will become the natural voice in your head.

Channel Your New Thoughts

Do something constructive or creative with your new thoughts and feelings. Do anything that reinforces this belief and expresses your new feelings. This will help you anchor that truth in your mind, body, and life. The goal here is to realize that you should always feel worthy regardless of the situations you're experiencing. You can draw, paint, dance, write, sing, or exercise - whatever feels natural and good to you. It also helps to do this activity when you feel negative thoughts or feelings arising. They can serve as a reminder that this negativity doesn't define you.

The body creates memories that you're not always aware of. Channeling your thoughts and feelings into constructive outlets allows your body to create positive associations. You'll immediately feel better when you associate healing activities like art, yoga, and breathing exercises with good feelings.

You don't have to immediately ambush your brain about why your negative thoughts aren't true. You can simply sit with them and feel them. Carry them and express them through your desired outlet. Your body will immediately pick up on the good feelings associated with the practice.

Suppressing and ignoring negativity makes it harder to recognize it. It sits in your subconscious long and brews. Incorporating constructive activities in your routine encourages your brain to make your new truths stand out. The positive beliefs will eventually become your first thoughts.

Changing How You Measure Your Self-Worth

Make a List of All Your Skills and Talents

Everyone has something to bring to the table. You may be an amazing artist, a talented athlete, or a great communicator. Don't underestimate your abilities. You may be inclined to think that the things you're good at aren't that impressive. However, something as simple as giving effective presentations or being an effortless negotiator isn't something everyone can do. These skills can help you significantly in your everyday life, especially when you need to get your point across or walk away with an awesome deal. Think about the things you offer the world and capitalize on them.

Forgive Yourself

Practice self-forgiveness and go easy on yourself for all your past mistakes and shortcomings. Understand that messing up is necessary for growth and development. Work on letting go of guilt and shame and build a positive, compassionate relationship with yourself.

Take Risks

Don't let your fear of failure and risk-taking stop you from pursuing new opportunities. Stop doubting your abilities to take on potential challenges and adapt to dramatic changes in your life. Jump at any chance that will allow you to become a better version of yourself.

Practice Self-Love

Learn to love yourself for who you are, regardless of your negative traits and qualities. Instead of ripping yourself apart, work on enhancing the thought processes or getting rid of these negative traits.

How you measure your self-worth impacts the quality of your life. Unhealthy measurement standards can take a toll on your mental, emotional, and physical health. Accepting that you're worthy regardless of your appearance, job, bank account, social network, and other material aspects will lead to a sense of fulfillment, better self-esteem, and, ultimately, satisfaction with your life.

Chapter 4: Changing the Script: How to Reprogram Your Mind

This chapter explores cognitive reframing and its benefits. You'll understand the harmful cognitive distortions people commonly experience and how they manifest. You'll also learn what neuroplasticity is, how to improve it, and how it can help you restructure your thought patterns. Finally, you'll learn 5 simple yet effective steps that will help you reframe your thoughts.

Reprogramming your mind can help you restructure thought patterns.
https://unsplash.com/photos/bwKtz4YVtmA?utm_source=unsplash&utm_medium=referral&utm_content=creditShareLink

Cognitive Reframing

Your thoughts determine how you perceive the world around you and can greatly impact how you behave. Often, thought patterns result from certain beliefs people have, which is why they result in unhealthy emotions and reactions. For instance, if you believe you're not skilled enough, you'll keep thinking about possibly losing your job or receiving negative evaluations. This can give rise to emotions like frustration and stress and even lead to anxiety and other mental health disorders. This hinders your ability to concentrate and do your best at work, further reinforcing the belief that you're not good enough.

Cognitive reframing is the process of reframing your thoughts to change how you perceive certain events and situations. It requires you to replace negative thought patterns with more positive and constructive ones. When you do this for long enough, your new thoughts will eventually become your standard way of thinking, improving your mental and emotional health and mood.

This process requires you to work on your self-awareness and bring your attention to your thought patterns. This way, you can catch harmful thoughts just as they begin to formulate so you can address them early on. The more you allow negative thoughts to stew in your mind, the more impact and power they'll have on your perceptions, mood, behaviors, and feelings.

You can also alter your stress response through cognitive reframing. Stress is associated with high cortisol levels and the initiation of the fight-or-flight response in the body. Any situation that you perceive as mildly threatening will initiate the stress response. For example, your heart rate may increase, you may start sweating or breathing more heavily, or you may experience chills because it's your body's way of dealing with high stress levels.

Learning to reframe your thoughts allows you to keep your stress levels at bay and lower your stress response. This technique helps you relax and encourages you to view the situation from different perspectives.

When addressing your negative thoughts, it helps to identify which type of cognitive distortion you're experiencing. Cognitive distortions are irrational thought patterns that can have jarring effects on your overall well-being. There are several cognitive distortions that many people experience every day. However, a high tendency toward these ways of thinking can lead to persistent negative feelings and unwanted behaviors and is linked to several mental health conditions. Understanding different cognitive disorders allows you to recognize when they arise so you can turn them into better thoughts.

The following are a few of the most common cognitive distortions that people experience:

All-or-Nothing Thinking

This type of cognitive distortion is characterized by the tendency to perceive only two possible outcomes of any situation. All-or-nothing thinkers believe that the outcome is either going to be brilliant and that everything will go their way or that everything will turn out to be horrible and that the worst possible scenario will occur.

There are very few situations in life where anything can be labeled as a completely good or successful outcome or a totally bad or failed result. Most situations exist on a spectrum with various factors affecting the outcomes and people's perceptions of them. People who experience all-or-nothing thinking usually miss out on these nuances and go through exaggerated thought patterns when the best-case scenario doesn't take place. For instance, an athlete who doesn't perform as well as they thought in a single competition may think they'll never amount to anything in their athletic journey.

Mind-Reading

This cognitive distortion is mostly experienced by people who struggle with social anxiety. Mind-reading refers to making assumptions and trying to guess what others think. These assumptions are usually negative and are backed with zero to little evidence. People who engage in this thought pattern are attentive to even the slightest verbal and non-verbal cues and interpret them as signs that the other person feels bored, annoyed, or frustrated with them.

For example, if someone with this cognitive distortion notices their friend glancing at their watch, they may see it as a sign that they're bored and want to leave. However, there are probably other explanations. They may be simply looking at the time or have an appointment or something important to do in a few hours.

Overgeneralization

Overgeneralization refers to the habit of thinking that what applies to a certain situation applies to all similar ones. You may think that they'll all lead to the same outcomes, keeping you from pursuing new opportunities and experiences. This will limit your personal growth and development and affect your professional and social life. People who overgeneralize might avoid seeing new people because they went on one bad date. They'll assume that they'll never find someone or that they're not good at dating.

Mental Filtering

Mental filtering refers to how someone directs their attention toward certain aspects of a situation. People who have this cognitive distortion usually pay attention to the bad aspects and overlook the good parts of any situation. This causes them to think that nothing is skewed in their favor and gives them an unrealistic perception of the world, which leads to ungratefulness and a negative mindset. For example, if a student receives one low grade, they may think they're failing academically. They'll disregard all the times they scored high grades on their tests and assignments, the great projects they worked on, and the amount of hard work they put into studying.

Cognitive reframing allows people to deconstruct and falsify these distortions. It requires you to catch negative thought patterns, address them, think about why your thoughts and beliefs are unrealistic, and reframe them into more positive and rational ones.

While it can be a long process that requires a lot of focus, effort, and determination, you can work on reframing your thoughts on your own. That said, speaking to a mental health professional, especially if you struggle with negative thoughts often, can be very helpful. CBT, or Cognitive Behavioral Therapy, is an approach that's particularly designed to help individuals recognize distorted ways of thinking and replace them with better and more helpful ones. CBT is commonly used for depression, substance abuse, marital problems, anxiety disorders, eating disorders, and other severe mental health conditions. Most of these conditions are caused or exacerbated by cognitive distortions and other unhealthy thought patterns.

Suppose you wish to start cognitive reframing on your own. In that case, you must familiarize yourself with how cognitive distortions affect your perception of the world. This will help you identify which type of cognitive distortion you're dealing with and catch it just as it starts to manifest. Many mindfulness techniques, such as mindful journaling and body scans, allow you to notice unwanted thoughts as they arise. When you're writing down your thoughts, you have a better opportunity to reflect on them and give yourself time to question their viability before acting on them. Journaling and body scanning can help you to differentiate between your original and true thoughts and the intrusive ones.

Why Cognitive Reframing Is Beneficial

Cognitive reframing can put your mind at ease and alleviate the symptoms of stress and anxiety. When you encounter challenging periods and stressful events, your initial reaction is usually negative. When they're frustrated and overwhelmed, very few people can see the cup half full. Giving into negative thought patterns and unhelpful ways of thinking can further exacerbate your feelings of stress._Learning to reframe your thoughts allows you to get rid of intrusive ideas and practice better emotional regulation, which can help you manage stress and anxiety.

For instance, if you have an upcoming first date that you're worried about, your mind may initially wander off to all your failed past experiences. You may even engage in negative self-talk and tell yourself that you will mess up and they'll never want to see you again. You'll make yourself feel even more anxious and walk into the date with the idea that you'll blow it either way. Through cognitive reframing, however, you can adopt more constructive thought patterns. You'll come to realize that your past experiences can't dictate the success of your upcoming date. You'll also get into the habit of reminding yourself that everyone has their fair share of unsuccessful dates.

Cognitive reframing can also boost your self-confidence and self-esteem. It gives you the tools to effectively challenge your negative thoughts and prevent self-deprecating talk. When you learn to have neutral, realistic, and even positive conversations with yourself, you'll start to notice your strengths and abilities.

If you struggle with low self-esteem, you may often criticize and tear yourself down. Whatever you say to yourself will eventually sound real. Your subconscious mind will believe if you tell yourself how inadequate or how much of a failure you are. The way you carry and introduce yourself will lack confidence. You'll expect to fail at everything you do, which will demotivate you from trying things properly. When you expect the worst, you'll do your worst and actually receive the worst outcomes, which will further reinforce the initial negative thought: "I'm a failure."

On the other hand, if you constantly repeat uplifting statements and positive affirmations to yourself, such as "I'm always enough" and "I'm capable of achieving anything I want," you'll start to believe it and act like it. You'll be self-assured and act confident that the outcome will be positive. You'll feel more motivated to work harder, which will get you the results you want.

Cognitive rewiring can also be beneficial for your social relationships. By identifying and reframing your negative thoughts, you'll stop making unhelpful assumptions about others and become more receptive and open toward them. For example, you'll stop paying attention to everything other people do and taking them as signs that they have negative feelings toward you.

Suppose you struggle with cognitive distortions and poor emotional regulation. In that case, you may assume that your co-worker is lazy or incompetent just because you don't like them or you made a negative first impression about them. Instead of being too judgmental, cognitive reframing teaches you to change your perception and become more tolerant. Instead of thinking they're incompetent, you'll tell yourself they're likely doing the best they can or are still learning.

Cognitive reframing can be used to deal with illnesses and physical pain. People who struggle with chronic illnesses and pains usually feel powerless, hopeless, and sorry for themselves. However, with cognitive reframing, they can change their mindset, which can even alleviate their pains and enhance their overall well-being. Someone with chronic pain, for instance, may think that their condition stops them from enjoying certain aspects of their life. When they rewire their negative thoughts, they'll see that they're slowly learning to manage their pain and still do things they like doing.

Neuroplasticity

Cognitive reframing is possible due to neuroplasticity, which is the brain's ability to be influenced, adapted, and changed by different experiences. It involves the reorganization, growth, and transformation of neural networks. Neuroplasticity could also be the result of brain damage or structural changes that occur in the brain due to learning.

The term "plasticity" is associated with the brain's adaptability and malleability, while "neuro" refers to the foundational nerve cells in the nervous system and the brain- neurons. While it was believed that the body stops creating neurons shortly after birth, new studies, according to Very Well Mind, suggest that the brain can create new neurons, rearrange its existing pathways, and make new connections.

Functional and structural plasticity are two types of neuroplasticity. The former refers to the brain's ability to transfer functions and processes that occur in the brain from damaged centers to healthier ones. The latter is the brain's ability to physically transform its structure due to learning.

Individuals experience a period of rapid cognitive growth during the earlier years of their lives. Upon birth, there are only around 2,500 synapses in the part of the brain known as the cerebral cortex. By the time a child turns three, this number grows to an estimated 15,000.

However, you may be surprised to learn that adults only have around 7,500 synapses per neuron, 50% of what they had during their early childhood. This is because as you grow up, you make new memories, learn things, and go through various experiences. These changes strengthen some connections in the brain and completely get rid of other ones. The strengthening and elimination of connections that happen with growth are known as synaptic pruning.

Naturally, the neurons you use or rely on the most in your day-to-day life end up having stronger connections. On the other hand, neurons that you rarely use or don't seem to need to die over time. Your brain adapts to the circumstances and environment by creating new connections, strengthening existing ones, and eliminating weak connections.

Neuroplasticity is a crucial characteristic of the human brain because it encourages it to adapt to external, as well as internal, changes, improves its ability to learn new things, and makes it possible to reinforce current cognitive abilities. It also helps the brain recover from severe medical conditions like strokes and brain traumas or injuries, enhances brain functions and health, and strengthens the parts of the brain that have declined with time.

How Neuroplasticity Helps with Cognitive Reframing

Neuroplasticity plays a key role in the cognitive reframing process, as it encourages the brain to build new neural pathways and create connections as people develop and practice new thought patterns. It guides the entire cognitive reframing process, from challenging old and unhelpful thought patterns to replacing them with better and more constructive ones. With enough practice, the brain rewires itself to adopt the newly developed new patterns as the standard way of thinking. The rewiring process happens when the brain strengthens certain connections, prunes or gets rid of other ones, and creates new neural associations.

Mindfulness techniques, an important aspect of CBT and cognitive reframing, can also improve a person's cognitive flexibility and enhance their emotional regulation skills. Mindfulness and cognitive techniques can support the brain's natural ability to change and adapt to certain stimuli and cues, improving cognitive reframing and enhancing neuroplasticity.

Characteristics of Neuroplasticity

Age and the environment in which people live play a great role in how neuroplasticity occurs, even though it can happen at any point during a person's life. Some types of plasticity happen more commonly at certain stages in life. For instance, during earlier childhood, the brain grows and develops on its own.

Brains are usually more responsive to environmental changes and are more sensitive during the early years of life compared to older individuals. In other words, while adult brains can adapt to experiences, younger brains are more responsive. A person's genetic makeup and how they interact with the surrounding environment also affect their brain's plasticity.

Plasticity happens continuously during a person's lifetime and isn't exclusive to neurons. It also happens to other cells in the brain, such as vascular and glial cells. However, the brain isn't entirely adaptable. Some parts are responsible for certain functions, such as speaking, understanding, and moving. If you experience a severe brain injury that affects one of the key areas, some functions will naturally be affected. During recovery, in some cases, it is possible for the healthy parts of the brain to take over the functions of certain other affected parts.

Improving Neuroplasticity

You can improve your brain's plasticity by enriching your environment, seeking out learning opportunities, and trying new experiences. Do things that stimulate your focus and test your problem-solving abilities. Challenges and a sense of newness can strengthen neural connections and lead to desirable cognitive changes.

You can go on adventures and travel to new areas, read, engage in creative activities like art or writing, or learn to play an instrument or speak a new language. Playing card, board, or even video games and engaging in mindfulness exercises can also help.

Ensuring that you're well-rested and get enough sleep every night is essential to your brain's growth and development. Sleep can strengthen the areas of the brain responsible for transmitting information among the neurons, which improves plasticity. Maintaining good sleep hygiene, going to bed and waking up at the same time every day, avoiding stimulating activities before bed, and setting up an ideal sleep environment can improve your overall mental and physical health.

Getting your fair share of exercise improves physical health and improves cognitive functions. Regular physical activity can reduce the risk of neuron loss in parts of the *hippocampus*, the part of the brain responsible for memory and learning.

Exercise impacts the brain-derived neurotrophic factor, which is a protein that influences nerve growth. Physical activity also stimulates the area of the brain associated with motor control, known as the basal ganglia.

How to Restructure Your Thoughts

Step 1: Practice Self-Monitoring

If you wish to change a certain thought pattern, you have to notice the thoughts and feelings associated with it. Take a step back and observe your mind and surroundings when these thoughts come up. Notice what words, actions, or situations triggered the onset of these thought patterns. Keep observing your thought process several times and start drawing connections.

For instance, if you often see yourself as a failure, pinpoint the situations that make you feel like this. Do people's words or perceptions affect how you feel about yourself, or do these thought patterns arise in a professional or academic setting? If so, is it something that your boss or teacher said, or are these thoughts a product of something else entirely?

Understanding your triggers allows you to take action and start rewiring your thoughts.

Step 2: Question Yourself

Questioning yourself plays a major role in dissipating symptoms of stress and anxiety. To effectively reframe your thoughts, you need to determine their validity. Identify whether they're based on evidence or emotions and if there are ways to test the accuracy of your belief.

In most cases, your thoughts will be exaggerated. Determine the cognitive distortion you're dealing with and its effect on your thought patterns. For instance, if you notice that you're overgeneralizing, you'll start to see that "I'm a failure" is an over-exaggerated statement.

Step 3: Obtain Evidence

Now that you realize that your thoughts are irrational, you should start gathering evidence that takes their power away. For example, you should think of all the times you handed in your work on time, the positive remarks you received, and the compliments you got from your co-worker and boss. Do you still think of yourself as a complete failure?

Step 4: Make a Cost-Benefit Comparison

Using this technique, you will weigh the pros and cons of maintaining your negative thought patterns.

Does this cognitive distortion help you physically and emotionally?

What will the long-term effects/consequences of this cognitive distortion be?

Do these thoughts impact your relationships with others or how people think of you? How so exactly?

Do these thoughts push you or limit you further?

Step 5: Come Up with Alternatives

Now that you know your thought patterns aren't serving you, it's time to brainstorm helpful ways to address your problem. For example, if you missed a deadline, think about why it happened. Did you bite off more than you could chew? Was it a time-management issue? How can you practice saying "no" to unreasonable requests or asking for deadline extensions if it's the former? How can you manage your time more effectively if it's the latter?

Cognitive reframing is a popular psychological technique that involves reframing your negative thoughts into more constructive ones to positively impact your perceptions of yourself and the world around you. Practicing cognitive rewiring can alleviate symptoms of stress and anxiety, improve your intrapersonal relationships, boost self-confidence, and even help manage chronic illnesses and pain.

Chapter 5: Mindfulness: How to Worry Less by Being in the Present

If you don't find a way to break free from it, anxiety can affect the balance of your life. The question is, how does one break free from this vicious cycle? The answer is simple: by practicing mindfulness.

Mindfulness is a meditation technique where you pay close attention to your internal thoughts and experiences without judging yourself.

This chapter touches on the various techniques of mindfulness that can free you of worries and improve your focus on the present. Focusing entirely on the present moment will lessen and even remove any feelings of anxiety and stress you may be struggling with. You will learn practical tools with scientific backing to integrate into your daily life.

What Is Mindfulness?

Mindfulness involves being completely conscious and engaging yourself in the present by having all your mental and physical being focused on what is happening in the moment. It involves paying attention to your thoughts and feelings as they develop and learning to watch them unfold without allowing them to occupy mental space.

Mindfulness and meditation can help you minimize overthinking.
https://unsplash.com/photos/Zf0-
90SpDD0?utm_source=unsplash&utm_medium=referral&utm_content=creditShareLink

You can practice mindfulness in many ways, including mindful breathing, eating, and walking in nature. The key to engaging and living in the present moment is to be aware of what you do at any given moment.

What Is the Relationship between Mindfulness and Overthinking?

One might ask, "How does mindfulness help with excessive thinking?" This answer lies in a complete understanding of what overthinking means. People overthink because they become engrossed in a certain idea without realizing it. When you allow worry, fear, or regret to take over, you will lose touch with the present and the truth of your surroundings.

Mindfulness is the perfect remedy for overthinking because it brings thoughts and feelings into your consciousness as they happen. That way, you can break free from the habit of getting overwhelmed by them. Mindfulness teaches you to objectively observe your thoughts without any attachment or judgment, which keeps you from being swept away by your inner mind. It also allows you to develop a stronger sense of perspective and clarity of mind. You even get to notice when you are caught up with overthinking habits.

What are some of the ways that mindfulness can assist with overthinking?

Here are just a handful of the advantages you will enjoy:

1. Reduced Anxiety and Stress

Cortisol is a hormone the body releases when it is under stress; numerous health conditions could result from it, including weight gain, high blood pressure, and a weak immune system. However, with mindfulness, you can reduce the release of cortisol in your body, ultimately leading to a healthy and happy life.

By noticing your thoughts without getting attached or judging, you can break the vicious cycle of concern and rumination that eventually leads to overthinking.

2. Increased Self-Awareness

Mindfulness can make you conscious of your thoughts and habits and get you to notice when you begin to overthink things. Using mindfulness, you can easily break out of the loop and see things positively.

3. Boosts Immune System

Practicing Mindfulness meditation makes you less vulnerable to disease and illness. When your stress and anxiety levels decrease, your body produces more killer cells that are essential for fighting infections.

4. Improved Attention and Concentration

Your capacity to focus and concentrate on the tasks you have at hand will improve more when you practice mindfulness and stay in the present.

5. Enhanced Emotional Resilience

Through mindfulness, you can create a stronger feeling of inner strength and resilience in the face of challenging situations. Instead of being overwhelmed by unpleasant thoughts and feelings, you can learn to recognize them without being engulfed by them.

6. Improved Sleep

Overthinking can interfere with your ability to get enough sleep, making you exhausted and cranky the following day. On the other hand, mindfulness helps you relax and unwind before bed, thereby lessening the impact of excessive thinking on your sleeping habits.

In 2014, Amber Hubbling and three others from the College of Pharmacy, University of Minnesota, USA, published their research in BMC Complementary and Alternative Medicine.

Their findings showed the impact of mindfulness training through meditation and yoga on chronic insomnia in adults. They found that mindfulness training increased the awareness of the thoughts and emotions of the test subjects. The study involved 18 adults who had undergone an 8-week mindfulness training program. After that, they were divided into groups and asked to share their experiences.

The participants testified that their mindfulness techniques positively affected their sleep quality and helped them manage their insomnia issues. They also observed an improvement in the subjects' sleep quality as well as their ability to handle insomnia. The subjects reported that they gained emotional and physical benefits from practicing mindfulness. They also found the group sessions motivating.

From those results, the researchers suggested that healthy sleeping habits and mindfulness education can benefit people with chronic insomnia.

Practicing Mindfulness

Your job, family, relationships, and other responsibilities can be quite overwhelming and may even leave you with anxiety and stress. However, practicing mindfulness is effective in helping you reduce excessive thinking and anxiety, manage stress, and achieve inner clarity and peace.

1. Mindful Breathing

Mindful breathing is a technique that involves paying attention to your breath and observing it without any judgment. It's a meditative practice that aids in maintaining awareness, presence, and serenity. It can also help you feel less stressed and anxious, clear your mind, and help you to feel better overall.

Hyunju Cho of the Department of Psychology, Yeungnam University, Gyeongsan-si, South Korea, published an article on the effectiveness of mindful breathing on Plos One in 2016.

The researchers investigated the daily effects of mindful breathing exercises and their effectiveness in relieving anxiety among university students. A total of 36 students, divided into groups, were involved in the study. While the first group practiced mindfulness breathing exercises in a bid to alleviate anxiety, the second group did a different kind of exercise. On the other hand, the third group did not participate in any exercise. This went on for about six consecutive days, and the students were asked to document their experience every day during the experiment. They were also given pre-training and post-training questionnaires to evaluate their perceptions of anxiety.

The results indicated that both mindful breathing exercises and alternative exercises reduced anxiety among students. Furthermore, the group that practiced mindful breathing exercises reported more positive thoughts than the others. These findings suggest that daily mindful breathing exercises can effectively reduce anxiety and promote positive thoughts.

The following are simple instructions to follow to practice mindfulness breathing:

- Find a comfortable chair or cushion to sit on. Keep your feet flat on the ground and sit with your back straight. You could also lie down if you want.

- Relax by keeping your eyes shut and taking a few deep breaths. Concentrate on your breathing and observe the sensation of your breaths as they enter and leave your nostrils. Notice how the air feels cool when you inhale and warm when you exhale.

- You can count your breaths to help you concentrate. Count from 1 to 10 as you inhale and exhale, and start again when you reach 10.

- While practicing mindful breathing, especially as a beginner, you will notice your mind drifting to thoughts that aren't important. When this happens, don't try to fight the thought; acknowledge it and gently bring your attention back to your breathing. Don't judge yourself for having those thoughts or being distracted; it is completely normal.

- To master mindful breathing, you need to practice it consistently. Try it for about 5 to 10 minutes each day. You can increase the duration as you become more comfortable.

Mindful Walking

Mindful walking is where you take slow, deliberate steps while staying conscious and in the moment. This exercise aims to cultivate mindfulness and get you to become aware and fully present in the moment.

The main difference between mindful and regular walking is that the former requires you to pay attention to every step you take, the sensation of the ground beneath your feet, and a complete awareness of your surroundings. This exercise will help you slow down and return to the moment instead of being engrossed by your concerns.

M. Teut from Institute for Social Medicine, Epidemiology and Health Economics, Charité-Universitätsmedizin Berlin, published an article in Evid Based Complement Alternat Med in 2013.

This study examined the effectiveness of mindful walking toward stress alleviation. The participants in the experiment were people between the ages of 18 and 65 who were experiencing high-stress levels. The researchers randomly divided the participants into two groups. The first group was made to practice the mindful walking exercise while the other group didn't do any exercises (as they were the waiting group).

The mindful walking group was made to engage in the exercise for 40 minutes, dedicating the first 10 minutes to just being in the moment. For the next 10 minutes, they were asked to focus entirely on their experiences. In the last 20 minutes, the group was asked to walk regularly. During the entire 4-week exercise, the other group (the waiting group) didn't do any exercises or activities.

By the end of the four weeks, the researchers made each group complete a survey to gauge their stress levels. The results showed that the group that participated in mindful walking reported less stress and improved quality of life, while the other group didn't show much difference in their stress levels compared to when they started.

Mindful walking is an exercise that you can carry out anywhere. The following are steps to practice mindful walking.

- **Find a quiet and peaceful location.** This can be a park, garden, or a quiet street. Most importantly, pick a place where you feel safe and at ease.

- **Stay still and take a few deep breaths.** Concentrate on your breathing and center yourself. Take a slow deep breath, and then exhale slowly.

- **Begin to walk slowly and steadily, focusing on each step.** Pay attention to the sensation of each foot as it touches the ground, your leg movements, and the rhythm of the breaths you take.

- **Observe the sights, sounds, and smells around you.** Stay entirely in the moment without judgment or distraction.

- **Stay focused on your body.** If you notice your mind wandering, gently bring your focus and concentration back to your body and the walking sensation.

- **Practice for at least 10 minutes.** Aim to exercise mindful walking for at least ten minutes or longer.

- **End with gratitude.** Take some time to show gratitude for the experience. You can say "thank you" silently or take a deep breath and appreciate the present moment.

The following tips can help you enhance the effectiveness of your mindful walking and increase your enjoyment:

- **Start with short walks:** Begin with short walks for a short period and gradually increase the duration, especially if you're new to mindful walking.

- **Turn off your phone:** Turn off your phone or put it on silent mode to reduce distractions.

- **Walking in nature:** Walking in nature can be calming and grounding. Find a park, forest, or beach if possible.

- **Focus on your breath:** Concentrating on your breath can help you stay focused and in the moment.

- **Notice your body:** Pay attention to the sensations in your body, like tension or discomfort, and adjust your posture accordingly.

- **Be patient.** To see results, take your time and be patient. If your mind wanders or the exercise becomes too challenging to focus on, don't worry. You will find it more comfortable the more you practice.

- **Practice regularly.** Make sure to engage in a mindful walking exercise at least once a day or as frequently as possible.

- **Use a mantra:** You can repeat simple mantras like "peace" or "calm" to stay focused and present during your walk.

Journaling/Expressive Writing

Journaling and expressive writing are effective in helping you practice mindfulness.

Andrea N. Niles and five other researchers published an article in June 2013 on expressive writing in Anxiety Stress Coping.

Their research examined the impact of expressing feelings through writing and how it impacts mental and physical health. The participants were adults split into two groups. One group was told to write down their most traumatic or stressful experiences or something totally unrelated for about 20 minutes – this was repeated four times.

The anxiety, depression, and physical symptoms of the participants were examined before and after the writing exercise. Results showed that writing significantly impacts depression, anxiety, and physical symptoms. It was also observed that expressing emotions through either verbal communication or other methods can also benefit from writing about their emotions. On the other hand, people who suppress their feelings and don't express them are bound to suffer anxiety.

The following are some ways journaling helps with overthinking and mindfulness:

- It creates a safe environment where you can express yourself without fearing judgment or criticism.
- It allows you to deeply explore your thoughts and feelings, which will lead to gaining new perspectives and insights.
- It helps you identify and challenge negative self-talk, replacing it with positive affirmations and realistic thinking.
- It prevents rumination by allowing you to process and release difficult emotions and experiences.
- It provides a sense of distance and perspective, helping you see situations from a more objective point of view.
- It reduces emotional distress by promoting mindfulness, relaxation, and self-compassion.

How to Practice Journaling

Having understood that journaling is a powerful tool that can help you overcome overthinking, let's look at the practice in detail.

The following steps can help you get started:

Step 1: Choose Your Format

Your very first step is to choose your preferred format. There are many available options, including:

- **Pen and paper** - This classic format is the best if you enjoy the actual writing experience by hand and want to disconnect from digital distractions.

- **Digital** - This is an ideal format for you if you prefer typing or want to save your journal entries to a device or the cloud.

- **Audio** - This is the perfect format for you if you prefer to say what you're thinking aloud or have difficulty writing or typing.

Step 2: Choose Your Time and Place

Your next step is to create a consistent routine you can commit to in the morning, during your lunch break, or even at night.

Also, choose a quiet and comfortable place that will allow you to focus on your Journaling without any distractions – it could be your bedroom, a coffee shop, or a cozy corner of your home.

Step 3: Set Your Intention

Before you even start journaling, you should take some time to set your intention for the session. Think about what you want to achieve through your Journaling. A few examples include:

- Reflecting on recent events or experiences

- Processing difficult emotions

- Brainstorming ideas for certain projects or goals

- Expressing gratitude or joy

Setting an intention will allow you to stay focused and motivated during your journaling exercise.

Step 4: Start Writing

Now it's time to start writing. Below are some tips and techniques that you can follow to get the most out of your journaling:

- Don't worry about grammar, spelling, or punctuation. Just let your thoughts flow without judgment or editing.

- Don't censor or sugarcoat your feelings. Allow yourself to be vulnerable but, most importantly, authentic.

- Write about your current thoughts – the things that are currently on your mind. Don't dwell on the past or worry about the future.

- Try different styles like bullet journaling, art journaling, or reflective journaling.

Step 5: Reflect and Review

When you've finished, take out some time and reflect on everything you have written down. What new thing did you learn about yourself? What revelations or insights did you get? When you reflect on your writing, you can better understand your behaviors and thoughts.

Consider reviewing the things you wrote every once in a while. That way, you can track your progress, identify recurring patterns or issues, and celebrate your achievements and growth.

1. Gratitude

Gratitude means showing appreciation for the good things in life, whether big or small.

Combining gratitude and mindfulness will give you a powerful tool to cultivate positivity, reduce stress, and improve your relationships.

Y. Joel Wong and other scientists from the Department of Counseling and Educational Psychology, Indiana University Bloomington, published an article in Psychotherapy Research in 2016.

The researchers conducted an experiment that involved 293 adults that were receiving therapy. These participants were divided into three groups. The first group was the control group, and they only received therapy. The second group received therapy and wrote down their inner thoughts and emotions about the stressful situations they experienced. The third group received therapy and wrote letters expressing their gratitude to others.

After 12 weeks of the intervention, the researchers found that those who wrote letters expressing gratitude reported feeling better than the other two groups. This shows that expressing thanks through writing can be good for your mental health and can be a useful part of therapy.

However, there was an interesting twist. The researchers found that using negative emotional words while writing made people feel worse than they already did. The participants who wrote down negative emotional words didn't experience the same degree of improvement as those who focused on expressing gratitude.

This study suggests incorporating writing letters or expressing gratitude into therapy can enhance mental well-being.

Here are some of the benefits of cultivating gratitude with mindfulness:

- You can increase your sense of happiness and well-being by concentrating on the good things in your life and savoring them with mindfulness.

- Mindfulness and gratitude enable you to shift your focus from negative thoughts and worries, thus, reducing your stress and anxiety.

- Being mindful of your interactions with others and expressing gratitude can improve your relationships and strengthen bonds.

- Gratitude has been linked to better physical health, a stronger immune system, lower blood pressure, and better sleep.

How to Practice Mindful Gratitude

Now that you've learned the benefits of mindful gratitude, let's teach you how to cultivate it. Here are some steps you can take to start practicing it in your daily life:

- **Start with Awareness**

The first step to practicing mindful gratitude is to be aware of the good things surrounding your life. Take some time out and reflect on what you're grateful for – a delicious meal, beautiful sunset, or a supportive friend.

- **Use Mindfulness to Savor the Moment**

After identifying one thing you're grateful for, savor it using mindfulness. Notice every sensation and detail and allow yourself to appreciate the entire experience.

- **Express Gratitude**

Don't be stingy with your words. Express your gratitude toward other people and show them that you appreciate them. You can write a simple note or share a smile. Expressing your gratitude will strengthen your relationship and spread positivity.

- **Practice Regularly**

Practicing mindful gratitude, like any habit, takes time and requires repetition. Make it a part of your regular daily routine. Set a couple of minutes aside each day to reflect on the things you're grateful for and savor the moment with mindfulness.

Mindfulness is a powerful tool that you can use to reduce worry and anxiety and improve your happiness and well-being. You can cultivate a greater sense of being in the present when you practice breathing, body awareness, mindful communication and activities, self-compassion, acceptance, and letting go of control and perfectionism.

Chapter 6: Stress Management: Strategies for All Life Sectors

Stress is a state in which you start worrying after facing a challenging situation. It's a natural response, and every human experiences it at different levels. It can be caused by anything ranging from a difficult work situation to difficulty managing a relationship. This chapter will focus on stress and anxiety, their differences, telltale signs, and strategies to apply in stressful situations.

Understanding Stress

Stress affects the mind and body differently depending on the person's physical and mental health. Although a bit of stress can motivate you to perform daily tasks, too much of it can cause several issues. Learning how to manage stress in different situations is crucial to make you feel less overwhelmed and perform better.

Too much stress can cause you to feel overwhelmed.
https://unsplash.com/photos/bmJAXAz6ads?utm_source=unsplash&utm_medium=referral&utm_content=creditShareLink

It's natural to feel stressed when dealing with daunting things like exams, job interviews, relationships, work, etc. For many people, the level of stress decreases naturally over time as they learn to deal with the situation effectively.

Understanding Anxiety

It's an emotional state where a person feels stressed and worried, putting the person into a poor state of mind with evident physical changes like increased blood pressure, sweating, heart rate, dizziness, and trembling.

The Difference between Stress and Anxiety

Stress and anxiety are often confused with each other because both are emotional responses caused by a challenging situation or trigger. While stress causes a person to experience similar symptoms of irritability, dizziness, fatigue, digestion issues, and sleeping disorders, which can go away after a short period, it only lasts for a short time span. On the other hand, anxiety is more of a persistent mental state where a person continuously worries, even when there is no trigger. In a nutshell, stress is a short-term response, whereas anxiety can linger for longer periods.

The Effects of Stress on the Body and Mind

Stress affects bodily function, behaviors, and emotions in several ways. These signs and symptoms are divided into physical, emotional, and behavioral categories. Here are some of the physical symptoms you can experience during stressful situations:

- Body aches and muscle pain
- Heart pounding and chest pain
- Feeling exhausted and having difficulty breathing
- Increased blood pressure
- Problems with digestion
- Weak immune system
- Feeling restless and having problems while sleeping
- Jaw clenching and muscle tension
- Feeling dizzy, shaky, and experiencing headaches
- Sudden weight changes

- Increased sweating

- Existing health problems become worse

Constant stress can lead to anxiety, depression, sadness, and panic attacks. It can easily trigger the following feelings:

- Getting overwhelmed even when doing the most mundane of tasks

- Impatience, anger, irritability

- Inability to appreciate good things

- Depression

Always feeling worried and tense Here are the behavioral changes you can expect to see in a person experiencing stress:

- Makes it challenging to decide, plan, and execute.

- It becomes increasingly challenging to concentrate on tasks.

- Snapping at people with or without reason.

- Being unable to remember things and decreased working memory.

- Nail biting.

- Overeating or losing appetite.

- Decreased sexual drive.

- Increased chances of using illicit drugs, smoking, or drinking alcohol.

- Distancing from friends, family, and peers.

These signs and symptoms can differ from one person to another. Likewise, the signs and symptoms mentioned above are also present in several other mental and physical health disorders and diseases. Therefore, it's crucial to consult your doctor or a certified healthcare professional to discuss the issues you are currently facing.

The Connection between Stress and Overthinking

While several things can trigger stress, a major contributor is overthinking. Although worrying is a part of life, overthinking past or future events can easily become stressful. People who overthink typically are stuck reliving the past, evaluating situations from different angles, and increasing their fears. That puts your health and well-being at risk, making you develop other mental problems like depression and anxiety.

Being constantly worried leads to an array of physical and mental health changes. It weakens the immune system and increases the chances of health issues related to the cardiovascular system. When a person overthinks, their brain gets trapped in a constant worry loop. Although there's no denying that some situations can make a person overthink, it's crucial to address them and take strategic steps to prevent that from happening.

Stress also affects a person physically. When stress levels are high, it increases your blood pressure which can lead to several cardiovascular issues down the line. Likewise, the immune system can get suppressed due to the surge of hormones and other chemicals produced under stress.

In an average person's life, there are four life areas where you can experience stress.

Work Stress

It's natural to experience stress in a work environment. Let's say you were working on a project at the office but encountered a few workflow hurdles that resulted in a delay. Not completing the project on time and facing challenges can turn into work stress.

Here are some techniques you can implement when dealing with work stress:

• Meditation

Mindfulness and meditation techniques are particularly helpful in tackling chronic stress triggered by work stress. Practicing them brings clarity to your thoughts, making you evaluate your actions without judgment and by focusing on present issues. When someone worries too much, disruptive thoughts can flood the brain and make them get stuck in their past thoughts. Effective breathing techniques are ways to relax the body and mind while reducing high stress levels. These techniques slowly improve your control over specific sensations and learn to reduce stress-inducing and worrying thoughts that linger in both the conscious and subconscious mind.

- Exercise

In the pursuit of stress management, you need to incorporate an exercise routine into your day. Keeping the body active through exercise reduces stress. Endorphins are released during physical activity, which are natural substances that act as mood boosters. These chemicals naturally reduce stress and induce a feeling of accomplishment that

- Identifying Stressors

Keep a small notebook and make it your habit to note down the situations at work which act as stressors, your response, and how you are addressing the situation. Noting down these stressors, your response, and how you responded can make you realize which situations trigger stress and the interventions you can make.

- Setting Boundaries

You need to maintain a work-life balance and set clear boundaries at the workplace. Define the rules around work to make your routine easier, more effective, and stress-free. For example, make it a rule not to check emails or workplace texts at home. Many fail to realize that blending work and life raises stress-inducing work-life conflicts. Simply following a schedule reduces this conflict while limiting stress.

- Developing Responses

Stress and overthinking can sometimes lead you to make unhealthy choices like consuming alcohol or illicit drugs. Instead of dealing with stress using these things, develop healthy responses like yoga, mindfulness meditation, or some form of exercise to stop overthinking and reduce tension.

These responses are not limited to physical activities only. Go out often with friends and family, explore new places, visit your loved ones, go on a hike, or simply lay on a couch while you read your favorite novel; the choice is yours. Besides incorporating these activities, work on improving your sleep routine if you are experiencing any issues because sleep naturally reduces the level of stress-inducing chemicals your brain accumulates over the day due to overthinking.

- Communicate Often

If you constantly face work stress, it's best to talk to your supervisor. The idea behind sharing these stress-inducing issues is to brainstorm on workplace issues and develop effective plans to potentially reduce them. The purpose of communicating is not to point out your problems but to find practical solutions to manage these stressors. Engaging in these discussions with your colleagues and management will clarify your current responsibilities, make you address challenges meaningfully, and make the workplace more comfortable.

- **Take Time Off**

Sometimes, continuous workload results in burnout and triggers chronic stress. Taking time off and disconnecting from work reduces stress, lets you think clearly, and find effective ways to tackle a particular situation. Go on a vacation, unwind from worries, and replenish your energy to perform at your best.

Relationship Stress

Excessive worrying or overthinking can negatively impact relationships, leading to various challenges. The propensity to dwell on past or future concerns can result in emotional unavailability in the present moment. The stress and anxiety from overthinking can also cause significant emotional distress. To navigate this effectively, consider the following stress management techniques:

- **Encourage Open Communication**

Open and honest communication with your partner is crucial. If you're feeling anxious or stressed about a situation related to your relationship, having a conversation with your partner can help clarify things. Share your concerns without asserting control or becoming confrontational. As you voice your worries, also make space to hear your partner's perspective. Understanding the situation's dynamics and being open to change can be instrumental in resolving issues.

- **Acknowledge Your Feelings**

Your feelings about an issue don't necessarily reflect reality. How you react to a certain situation can lead to overthinking and clouded judgment. For instance, you may feel that your partner no longer loves you because they seem more distant, but this could be due to other factors such as increased work pressures. Recognizing your feelings and the larger context can clarify most issues and help prevent excessive thinking.

- **Express Your Expectations**

Being transparent about your feelings and expressing your expectations to your partner can simplify things. Holding back doubts can lead to overthinking and stress. If you find yourself consumed with negative thoughts, challenge these doubts with evidence. Openly discussing your expectations can help alleviate unnecessary worries.

- **Prioritize Self-Care**

Taking care of your physical and mental health is crucial. Engaging in self-care activities like reading a book over Sunday morning coffee or going on sight-seeing adventures with friends can lift your spirits and stimulate endorphin production, reducing stress. Including your partner in activities you enjoy can also strengthen your relationship and help you move past any lingering doubts from past relationships.

- **Establish Clear Boundaries**

Many relationship stressors can be managed effectively by setting and communicating clear boundaries with your partner. For instance, if your partner wants to spend more time together, designate specific hours for this and explain respectfully why you cannot be available all the time. Clear boundaries can prevent misunderstandings and reduce stress.

- **Seek Support When Needed**

There may be times when you can't alleviate relationship stress on your own. In situations where you and your partner struggle to find common ground, seeking support from family members or close friends can be helpful. A different perspective can often shed light on issues and offer potential solutions.

Home/Family Stress

Home and family stress can be particularly challenging for chronic worriers and over-thinkers, as it can trigger a lot of anxious thoughts and feelings. Here are some stress management techniques that can help manage home and family stress while keeping the chronic worrier/over-thinker in mind:

- **Identify the Stress**

It can be anything from a relationship conflict to managing the household. Identifying the problem brings you one step closer to finding an effective strategy. While managing household chores and dividing them between family members may not be an issue, tackling serious family issues and conflicts can keep the stress levels over the roof, further clouding your brainstorming capabilities. In such situations, be open and talk with a trusted friend or see a therapist to overcome the stress and develop an effective action plan.

• Practice Self-Compassion

Seeing something not working out your way leads to stress. People who overthink and see issues failing to work out as planned are usually hard on themselves. This mindset is destructive and can result in anxiety, depression, and other health-related issues. Instead of punishing yourself mentally, practice self-compassion, be kind to yourself, and be open to opinions. Incorporate these positive approaches in your life, and you'll slowly feel less impacted by these issues.

• Be Realistic

It's best to talk with your family members when setting expectations. Maintain a realistic approach and set expectations they can fulfill. Talking with family members and being realistic about a particular situation simplifies matters and provides more control. It also gives a sense of relief as everyone realistically addresses the situation. People who think too much are prone to setting unrealistic expectations of others, which further triggers feelings of failure and disappointment.

The easiest way to set realistic expectations is by breaking a large task into manageable milestones. For example, if the entire home needs cleaning, setting an unrealistic expectation like cleaning it in one day is nearly impossible. Instead, break the cleaning process into several days. Doing this will provide a sense of accomplishment, keep you motivated as you achieve a milestone each day, and reduce stress.

• Communicate Openly and Honestly with Family Members

Holding back from your family members will only increase conflicts. Always be open and honest when communicating with your family. Encouraging family communication reduces conflicts and lets family members talk about sensitive issues. Remember to be empathetic and open to other perspectives when discussing these issues.

• Seek Professional Support

Certified healthcare professionals will guide you in exploring different possibilities and ways to manage stress caused by these issues. Your therapist will evaluate your mental health and suggest an effective method like cognitive behavioral therapy, family therapy, or anything else they see fit.

Money Stress

Financial instability – and several other problems related to managing finances – are some of the other stress-inducing problems in life. Money is a major stressor for everyone these days. Whether you are struggling to pay off your debt or have a financial obligation to fulfill for your family, these issues take stress levels to a chronic level. You can practice the following money management techniques to reduce the amount of stress you deal with because of financial issues.

- **Follow a Set Budget**

When dealing with money stress, the first step is to create your budget. Spending money without dividing the expenses adequately will only result in financial stress. Creating a budget will simplify the spending process and ensure you are spending on areas that will have better outcomes. It also aids in cutting down unnecessary expenditures and for better planning the future. You can start by listing your expenses and total income. Then move on to allocate a specific amount on these separately listed expenses. After allocating these expenses, evaluate and see whether you can reduce these expenses further. If you have some budget left to allocate, save it for a rainy day.

- **Controlling Situations**

While tackling these financial issues is challenging and can trigger a feeling of being out of control, focusing on what you can achieve is the way forward. For example, if you have already created a budget but are failing to manage expenses, evaluate your spending habits and budget to reduce stress and anxiety levels.

- **Seek Financial Advice**

If you still can't manage your budget, sharing these financial issues with your family or close friends can be beneficial. They may have some money-saving tips to share or could assist you in creating a feasible budget. You can also consult a financial advisor who can make a personalized budget for you and let you explore different strategies that can address your financial obligations.

- **Practice Gratitude**

When it comes to money, changing your perspective can make things easier and relieve stress. Reflecting on the things you appreciate can increase your gratitude and appreciate the goodness and positivity that surrounds you. Giving to charity or doing volunteer work are other ways of practicing gratitude.

- **Develop a Plan**

While creating a budget can help you to manage everyday expenses, having a long-term financial plan is crucial. For example, if you want to pay the remaining debt you took or the mortgage on time, developing a plan will make your life much easier.

Experiencing stress is an inherent part of human life. It is a natural response to people's diverse daily challenges and demands. Stress can be prompted by a wide array of situations, ranging in intensity from minor inconveniences to major life crises. These triggers can include anything from a simple traffic jam that makes you late for an appointment to more serious events such as job loss, illness, or a family crisis.

It's important to note that stress is highly individualistic. What may be a stressor for one person could be insignificant to another. For instance, public speaking could trigger immense stress for someone who is introverted or shy, while it could be a thrilling experience for someone else who thrives on being in the spotlight. The same goes for other stressors, such as social events, deadlines, or even certain environments. This variability is due to individual differences in personality, life experiences, coping strategies, and even genetic factors.

Understanding your personal stressors is a crucial first step toward managing stress. Self-awareness can help you identify what situations or events trigger stress for you. Regularly checking in with yourself and paying attention to signs of stress can help you in this process. These signs could be physical (like headaches or stomach aches), emotional (such as feeling overwhelmed or irritable), or behavioral (like changes in sleep or eating habits).

Once you've identified your stressors, you need to acknowledge and accept the stress they cause. Stress is not inherently negative - it's a normal reaction that can sometimes even be beneficial, such as when it provides the motivation to meet a deadline or the adrenaline to respond to danger. Embracing the situation doesn't mean you have to like it or resign yourself to suffering. Instead, it means acknowledging your feelings without judgment and recognizing that feeling stressed is okay.

Effective stress management is essential to mitigate the potential negative impacts of stress on your mental and physical health. Chronic stress can contribute to various health problems, including mental health disorders like depression and anxiety, cardiovascular disease, digestive problems, weakened immune systems, and cognitive issues like memory and concentration problems.

There are many strategies to manage stress effectively. One of the most straightforward is regular exercise, which can reduce stress hormones and stimulate the production of endorphins, your body's natural mood lifters. Another is maintaining a healthy diet, as poor nutrition can exacerbate your body's stress response.

Mindfulness and relaxation techniques, such as meditation, deep breathing, and yoga, can also greatly reduce stress. These practices can help you stay focused on the present moment, reducing worries about the past or future that can contribute to stress.

Another key aspect of stress management is maintaining a strong support network. This could include family, friends, or professionals like therapists or counselors. Having someone to talk to can provide a different perspective, offer advice, or simply provide a sympathetic ear.

It's also crucial to make time for rest and relaxation. This could mean taking a walk in a natural environment, enjoying a hobby, reading a book, or any other activity that brings you joy and relaxation.

Everyone experiences stress, and it's okay to ask for help if it becomes overwhelming. With understanding, acceptance, and effective management, stress can be navigated successfully, eventually contributing to personal growth and resilience.

Chapter 7: The Dark Mind: How to Deal with Negative, Dark Thoughts

Do you ever feel like your mind is a haunted house, with every dark thought ready to come at you any second? Maybe you think there's no escape from the dark, intrusive thoughts you get and believe this makes you a bad or mentally unstable person. However, that's not true at all. Many people who struggle with a dark mind have experienced these intrusive thoughts and negative emotions. The worst thing about this experience is that they feel completely and utterly alone. Dark thoughts can make you feel suffocated and drained and be downright terrifying sometimes. However, you don't have to deal with them forever, and you definitely don't have to deal with them alone.

Negative thoughts can sometimes feel like an inescapable, dark room.
https://unsplash.com/photos/B7XNN9uNAh8?utm_source=unsplash&utm_medium=referral&utm_content=creditShareLink

The worst thing about dark and intrusive thoughts is their unpredictable nature. They can come from anywhere, whether provoked or unprovoked. Although people believe that they only arise from traumatic events or triggering situations, they are often the result of inexplicable circumstances. Maybe they are a result of a traumatic event you experienced, or maybe they accumulated because of a series of events. Whatever the case, these thoughts can be so debilitating that they lead you to withdraw from your friends and family.

When dark thoughts take over, it seems impossible to escape. You may even feel stuck; no matter how hard you try, you can't break your unhealthy thought patterns. However, the good news is that there's a way out. You will have to implement the right strategies, but with practice and determination, there's really nothing you can't achieve. In fact, patterns of negative thinking and dark thoughts can be attributed to a particular mental health disorder, in which case, you should definitely seek professional help. On the other hand, if these dark thoughts are coming out of nowhere, there are multiple approaches you can take to tackle them.

Once you understand the psyche behind these thoughts, it will be much easier to deal with them directly. This chapter will provide you with how you can do this, and it doesn't just include clinical advice and on-paper strategies but also lets you know that you're not alone. Whether you're someone who deals with negative and dark thoughts daily or who's been having difficulty managing your thoughts after a recent event, this chapter is for you. Hopefully, by the end of it, you'll have a better grip on your intrusive thoughts and negative thinking patterns.

The Stigma Surrounding Dark Thoughts

Having a dark mind can feel like having a heavy storm cloud over your head that follows you wherever you go. Dark emotions can range from being stressed, sad, or pessimistic to being more intense and even having dangerous ideas. For example, do you sometimes think, "What if I swerved into oncoming traffic right now?" Or maybe you get thoughts like, "I'm not good enough," or "Maybe my friends would be better off without me." These are typical examples of dark thoughts; almost everyone has to deal with them occasionally. However, for some people, these thoughts can start becoming frequent and overwhelming. That is when they start to affect their daily lives. For instance, if a student who has been struggling in school gets frequent thoughts like, "I'm not good enough to get into a college" or "I'm not smart enough to succeed," this person will ultimately start to believe their thoughts. These thoughts can make anyone feel hopeless and miserable, making it even harder for the person struggling with this to focus on their studies or improve their performance in school.

The reality of negative thoughts is that everyone experiences them, and they can even be considered a normal part of life. Normal negative thoughts can range from mild self-doubt to feelings of loneliness. However, this issue starts to get serious when you start experiencing extremely negative or dark thoughts. More often than not, people feel embarrassed to talk about these feelings, especially when they're constantly bombarded with messages to be happy and positive all the time. The stigma that surrounds dark thoughts is what can make talking about these experiences a difficult process. You might feel weak – or even *terrible* – for having these thoughts, and therefore, not share these feelings with anyone, not even your loved ones. However, you should know that having dark thoughts doesn't make you a bad person, nor does it make you weak. In fact, feeling guilty about having these thoughts is proof enough that you have a conscience and are a good person. Acknowledging and addressing these thoughts is the first step toward improving mental health.

For many people, sharing these thoughts doesn't come easy, and for good reason. Take someone struggling with anxiety and finally find it within themselves to share it with their friend or parents. Instead of addressing their issue, accepting this person for who they are, or trying to help with their issues, their parents/friends neglected their complaints and gave unhelpful responses like, "Just snap out of it," or "It's all in your head." These kinds of dismissive comments can make a person feel even more alone and can even make them revert back into their shell. Unfortunately, experiences like this are all too common, making it scary for people to open up about their mental health issues to get the help they need.

The Science Behind Dark Thoughts

Do you ever find yourself asking what's wrong with you for having these dark thoughts? Do you ever wonder where they even come from? From overthinking worst-case scenarios to imagining terrible things happening to loved ones, the human mind can conjure up some pretty disturbing situations, but why do you get these thoughts in the first place? From a purely evolutionary perspective, negative thoughts are meant to serve an important purpose. The human brain is wired to focus on potential environmental threats and dangers so that people can stay alert and avoid harmful situations. In fact, it's scientifically proven that the human mind is more responsive to negative stimuli than positive stimuli, which is why negative thoughts grab more attention and stay in your mind longer.

In the modern world, humans do not have to face the uncertainty and dangers they used to. However, the brain still interprets non-threatening situations that are potentially dangerous, which can activate the part of your mind responsible for overthinking and excessive worrying. Undoubtedly, this was a helpful human response in the past, but today, it can be somewhat detrimental to your mental health. You should note that everyone experiences negative thoughts occasionally, but when these thoughts become persistent and intense, this can be a symptom of mental illness.

If you are experiencing persistent negative thoughts or emotions, seek help from a mental health professional. They can assess your symptoms and help you develop a treatment plan that meets your unique needs.

From a scientific, or specifically, a neurological perspective, negative thoughts can activate certain parts of the brain that are associated with emotional regulation. The amygdala, associated with emotional processing, can become hyperactive in people with anxiety, depression, or other mental disorders. This hyper-activeness results in people feeling more responsive to negative stimuli than normal people, and hence, they feel more intense negative emotions along the lines of fear, sadness, suicidal tendencies, etc.

Intrusive Thoughts: Understanding the Different Types

As a negative thinker, you've probably dealt with intrusive thoughts on multiple occasions. These thoughts are usually unwanted and distressing ideas or images that pop up in your head without any warning. Often, they can be disturbing, taboo, or weird, and having them makes you feel embarrassed or guilty. These thoughts can either be fleeting or stay in your mind for days on end and mostly come out of nowhere, which is why it's so hard to figure out how to deal with them. Maybe you've found yourself wanting to do something you don't want to, like hurting someone you care about, cheating on your partner, or saying something inappropriate in public. These are all examples of intrusive thoughts. They can be alarming if they increase in frequency and may even make you feel like a bad person for having them. However, you should remember that many people experience intrusive thoughts, and this experience is also linked to some mental illnesses. These can include:

1. Obsessive-Compulsive Disorder (OCD) Intrusive Thoughts

Intrusive thoughts when dealing with OCD can look like this: You're walking down the street, but suddenly you get an intrusive thought that you left the stove on at home and that your house will burn down. Even though you remember that you turned the stove off, the thought won't go away, and you start doubting your memory. This keeps nagging at you until you turn around and return to your house to check the stove.

This is just a common example of what intrusive thoughts in OCD can look like. These thoughts make you feel anxious and result in the disruption of your daily life. They might seem like small worries, but they can interfere with your ability to function properly when they happen frequently. Other examples of intrusive thoughts in OCD can include:

- An irrational fear that you will hurt someone, even though you have no intention of doing so.
- A fear of contamination from either germs or chemicals.
- You're scared that you'll lose control of your body while driving or when you're standing at the edge of a building.

While these thoughts can be very disturbing and difficult to manage, you should remember that they do not reflect who you are as a person. Your mental illness is not your entire personality.

2. Post-Traumatic Stress Disorder (PTSD) Intrusive Thoughts

If you've been in a traumatic situation that has left you with symptoms of post-traumatic stress disorder, then you most probably have also dealt with the intrusive thoughts that come with this disorder. Dealing with these intrusive thoughts can feel like being stuck in a never-ending horror movie. The scenes and images from your traumatic event play repeatedly in your head, which causes further emotional and mental distress. These thoughts can make you feel like you're reliving those stressful moments all over again. They can be triggered by sounds, smells, similar situations, or even passing thoughts.

For instance, a war veteran may get intrusive thoughts about gunfire or bomb explosions, and these may be triggered by loud noises or sudden movements. Similarly, a survivor of sexual assault may experience flashbacks of the event and intrusive thoughts about hurting themselves. Even seemingly small things like a certain song or a particular smell can bring back painful memories for people. PTSD intrusive thoughts can also manifest as feelings of shame and guilt. For instance, survivor's guilt can result in dark intrusive thoughts that can have you questioning whether you could have done something differently to prevent the traumatic event or help others.

Sometimes, these intrusive thoughts can result in avoidance behaviors, where you will try to avoid any situation that even poses to trigger your thoughts or memories. However, this can lead to social isolation and may inhibit your functioning skills for everyday life. You should always remember that experiencing PTSD or the intrusive thoughts that come with it does not make you weak, but you should seek professional help in case your symptoms leave you unable to function properly.

3. Generalized Anxiety Disorder (GAD) Intrusive Thoughts

Intrusive thoughts are quite sneaky in the sense that they can come out of nowhere and without warning. Before you know it, you're stuck with an intrusive thought that does not make sense but is unwilling to go away. You may have thought about something bad happening to your loved ones, something that hasn't even happened yet, or just fixated on past mistakes. For instance, you may be walking down the street, and suddenly, you start getting thoughts like, "What if I was hit by a car?" or "What if a speeding bus hit me?" You know it's not likely to happen, but the intrusive thought won't leave you alone. Maybe you suddenly think about an embarrassing moment you had in the past and spend the rest of the day thinking about this event instead of getting any work done.

These negative thoughts can be exhausting and can make you feel trapped in your mind. They also result in feelings of fear and anxiety, which can significantly impact your mental health and how you go about your day. Everyone has intrusive thoughts sometimes, but when these thoughts become overbearing and start to affect your ability to function properly, you know it's become a problem. In this case, you might be experiencing Generalized Anxiety Disorder (GAD).

Intrusive thoughts linked with this mental health disorder tend to be persistent and often repetitive. You'll find yourself worrying about things others consider unlikely or irrational. You may often imagine the worst-case scenarios in every situation, and these thoughts result in an overall feeling of doom and gloom, which is why you might find it hard to enjoy the present moment. If any of this sounds familiar, get a diagnosis, and maybe you'll have the answer to many of your problems. There are many ways to manage GAD and the intrusive thoughts that come with it. Just remember that you're not alone, and seeking help is never a sign of weakness.

How to Identify Intrusive Thoughts

Most people have experienced intrusive thoughts, overthinking habits, and negative thought patterns. Many types of thoughts can be considered intrusive. However, assuming that every negative thought you have is intrusive isn't how you should go about identifying your problems. So, how can you tell if a thought is intrusive or not? Well, here's a creative way to think about it:

Think of your thoughts as guests at a house party. The house is your brain, and some guests are welcome because they bring laughter, fun, and good conversation, while others show up uninvited, barge in without warning, make a mess of things, and refuse to leave. Those uninvited guests are your *intrusive thoughts, and* they can be dangerous or just plain annoying. Like bad guests, they can spoil your mood and the entire party. To tell if a thought is an uninvited guest or just a passing visitor, consider these tips:

- Notice the frequency of the thought. If it comes to your mind repeatedly, more than the others, even when you push it away or try to distract yourself, it may be an intrusive thought.

- Notice the emotion that comes with the thought. Intrusive thoughts usually bring a barrage of negative emotions with them, including guilt, shame, anxiety, fear, or sadness. You may feel like you're losing control or even going crazy when you have these thoughts.

- Consider the content of the thought. Intrusive thoughts usually contain varying and disturbing themes like danger, death, or sexuality. If a thought seems out of character for you, it may be intrusive.

Coping Strategies for Dealing with Dark Thoughts

Dealing with dark and intrusive thoughts can really make you feel alone. You probably think that no one else can understand your despair and what you're going through. However, know that you're not alone in this, and there are many coping strategies and techniques you can employ to deal with these thoughts. Maybe you find yourself zoning out during the day and being lost in your negative thoughts, or perhaps your dark thoughts have taken over, and you cannot even get out of bed to deal with life. Whatever the case, know that you're not a lost cause and that you will eventually find your way out of the darkness and into the light! Here are some coping techniques that will help you deal with your dark thoughts and provide a sense of relief:

1. Grounding Techniques

Do you suddenly panic when your dark thoughts refuse to leave your mind? Maybe some repetitive, intrusive thought keeps showing up inside your head for no reason. This is where a grounding technique can come in handy. These exercises help you gain control over your mind and bring you to the present moment instead of being stuck in your thoughts. The 5-4-3-2-1 exercise is a fun and effective grounding technique you can use whenever you start to drown in your dark thoughts:

- Take a deep breath and glance around the room to find five things you can see. It could be anything, from furniture to books, to paintings, or people. Focus on each of these 5 things and notice their details.

- Next, search for 4 things you can touch. Maybe it's the fabric of your shirt, the texture of your hair, or the surface of a nearby table. Pay close attention to how these textures feel against your skin.

- Then, identify 3 things you can hear. Maybe there's some music playing in the room, or you can hear birds chirping outside. You might even hear the hum of the AC if you listen closely.

- Now, find 2 things that you can smell. This one's a little tough, but you'll definitely find a particular aroma if you focus hard enough. Maybe you can smell food cooking nearby, the smell of the rain, or the fragrance of someone's perfume.

- Finally, find something you can taste. Maybe you have some gum lying around or a bag of chips nearby, and even a sip of water would do the trick. Pay attention to its taste and how it feels in your mouth.

Grounding techniques are perfect for bringing your attention back to the present moment and getting negativity out of your head. Once you've calmed down and escaped your negative thoughts, you can truly enjoy the beauty of life in the little things.

2. Journaling

If you feel that you have no one to talk to about your struggles and no one to share your dark thoughts with, then you should journal to ease your mind. Here are some prompts you can follow:

- List down any and all intrusive thoughts that come to you. Don't be afraid of judgment, as this journal should only ever be read by you.

- Once you've finished writing your thoughts, try to view them with curiosity instead of judgment.

- Identify any patterns, themes, or triggers that emerge from your thoughts. You'll surely find out some triggers which you can then avoid.

Remember that this technique is not an alternative to getting professional help if you're dealing with mental disorders. However, journaling does help you feel a lot lighter, especially when you feel like you don't have anyone to lean on.

3. Affirmation Jar

An affirmation jar will provide supportive statements when you need them the most. To make an affirmation jar, take some paper strips and write down positive affirmations or quotes that resonate with you. The more personalized these statements are, the better this technique will work for you. Fold up the paper strips after writing down affirmations and put them in the jar. Here are some phrases you can use in your affirmation jar:

- I am worthy of love and respect.
- I am capable of handling anything that comes my way.
- I trust myself to make the right decisions.
- I am enough just as I am.
- I am deserving of happiness and joy.
- I am constantly growing and learning.
- I am strong and resilient.
- I am capable of achieving my goals.
- I am in control of my thoughts and emotions.
- I am surrounded by love and positivity.

Whenever you're struggling with thoughts about self-doubt or feeling ashamed for having intrusive thoughts, take a piece of paper out, and read the affirmation to yourself. Repeat the statement as many times as it takes for you to believe it. This will interrupt your negative thought cycle and help you feel more in control of your thoughts and emotions.

Dark thoughts can be a formidable foe, but you can learn to conquer them with the right tools and mindset. Whether you turn to meditation, grounding techniques, or a good old-fashioned affirmation jar, there's no shortage of ways to shift your focus toward positivity and light. Remember that you are a wonderful individual with strengths and abilities that are uniquely your own. Don't be afraid to experiment, try new things, and find what works best for you.

Chapter 8: Time and Energy Management

"Your greatest asset is your earning ability. Your greatest resource is your time." -Brian Tracy

In a world of constant distractions, time and energy management is vital for the pursuit of happiness and success, but it becomes even more important if you are an over-thinker. People who overthink usually struggle with time and energy management skills due to impulsiveness and their ability to get distracted. Time and energy are finite resources, and strategically managing them can save you from wasting them on trivial things. This chapter provides practical tips and strategies for using your time and energy to achieve your fullest potential.

Time and energy management can help you achieve your potential.
https://unsplash.com/photos/BlIhVfXbi9s?utm_source=unsplash&utm_medium=referral&utm_content=creditShareLink

Why Are Time and Energy So Important to Mental Health?

Time and energy stand as the bedrock of maintaining mental health. Achieving a harmonious balance between the two can catapult you toward a realm of inner peace and satisfaction. Here's an elaboration on this concept:

1. **Time Fosters Self-Care:** Self-care has emerged as a necessity in your chaotic world to nurture and sustain mental health. Self-care practices can be as simple as enjoying a tranquil walk in the park, immersing yourself in a book, or meditating. Devoting just fifteen minutes of your day to such activities can significantly help in stress management.

2. **Time Facilitates Connection with Others:** Investing time in relationships with friends, family, and colleagues nurtures meaningful bonds. This sense of connection fosters a feeling of belonging and purpose, crucial elements in promoting mental well-being.

3. **Time Allows for Essential Breaks:** The monotony of work can sometimes be overwhelming, necessitating a step back to rejuvenate. Allocating time for rest is essential to provide your mind and body with a much-needed respite, helping you to regain vitality and alleviate work-related stress.

4. **Energy Inspires Exploration:** Abundant energy equips you with the capacity to venture beyond the routine, engaging in new or creative pursuits that infuse joy and fulfillment into your life. Embracing new experiences outside your comfort zone enhances self-esteem and confidence.

5. **Energy Enables Engaged Living:** Greater energy often leads to heightened productivity, infusing life with purpose. Pursuing a new language, nurturing a hobby, embarking on a business venture, or volunteering in your community can expand your skills' horizons. Such ventures help you actualize your dreams and unlock your latent potential.

6. **Energy Aids in Stress Management:** Misdirected energy toward unproductive activities can deplete and overwhelm you. Strategically planning your tasks can conserve energy, enabling

you to navigate unforeseen challenges. This approach ensures you handle any incoming responsibilities without succumbing to exhaustion.

7. **Time and Energy Boost Productivity:** A report from the U.S. Department of Health and Human Services found that individuals who were well-rested and judicious with their energy outperformed those who worked incessantly. Reserving time and energy, even in small measures, can mitigate stress and anxiety while enhancing productivity.

8. **Time Offers Space for Reflection:** The allocation of time for self-reflection is crucial for mental health. It permits introspection, allowing you to understand your thoughts and emotions better. This understanding can improve emotional intelligence, leading to better relationships and increased self-awareness.

9. **Energy Promotes Physical Well-Being:** Energy isn't just for mental pursuits; it's also vital for physical health. Regular exercise, good nutrition, and adequate rest can boost your energy levels, positively impacting your mental well-being. Physical health and mental health are interconnected, with improvements in one often leading to enhancements in the other.

The Importance of Time and Energy for Over-thinkers

The crucial role of time and energy management becomes even more pronounced for individuals prone to overthinking. Mismanagement in these areas often correlates to heightened stress and worry, leaving over-thinkers grappling with deadlines, struggling to complete tasks, and feeling overwhelmed by life's demands. The following factors shed light on this relationship:

Over-thinkers struggle with time and energy management because of their difficulty maintaining focus. Anxiety and tension can easily sidetrack the mind, causing it to stray into a labyrinth of unrelated thoughts. This diversion impedes productivity, draining both time and energy. According to a Journal of Business Research report, individuals under significant stress struggle to concentrate on their work, which detrimentally affects their productivity.

Another contributing factor is fatigue and burnout. Over-thinkers, often burdened by chronic stress and anxiety, frequently battle exhaustion. This physical toll can diminish motivation and interest in task completion. A study in the Journal of Occupational Health Psychology revealed that over-thinkers experiencing job-related stress are more susceptible to fatigue and burnout, undermining their ability to manage time and energy effectively.

In addition to these factors, disorganization in personal schedules, homes, or offices can exacerbate time and energy management struggles. Cluttered surroundings can feel overwhelming, hindering focus and motivation. According to a study in the Journal of Applied Psychology, employees in chaotic workplaces are more likely to experience burnout, negatively impacting their productivity.

Despite these challenges, there are strategies over-thinkers can adopt to enhance their time and energy management:

- Embrace mindfulness and relaxation techniques
- Cultivate a regular, consistent sleep routine
- Break down large tasks into smaller, more manageable parts
- Utilize digital tools like calendars, planners, and to-do list apps to stay organized

The correlation between stress, worry, time, and energy management is complex and multifaceted without a singular solution. Actively managing stress and overthinking through these methods can assist in handling work and daily chores more effectively, reducing overall stress and anxiety.

It's vital to remember that excessive stress, overthinking, and worry can be symptomatic of underlying mental health conditions like anxiety disorders or depression. If you experience these symptoms, seeking professional medical assistance is crucial.

Time Management Tips

1. Make a To-Do List:

As an over-thinker, becoming entangled in a web of anxieties, worries, and doubts is easy. The prospect of completing tasks can seem overwhelming. In such instances, a to-do list can be invaluable.

Formulating a daily to-do list allows you to break down tasks into smaller, more manageable portions, giving you a sense of control over your day and minimizing distractions and overthinking. It also provides a roadmap for your day, enabling you to adjust based on your progress as needed. Above all, it's an excellent tool to stave off procrastination and adhere to your schedule.

When creating your list, it's important to be realistic and specific. Instead of generalizing tasks such as "reading," break it down further to "read chapter 6 of the science textbook" or "spend 45 minutes completing today's homework." This approach will help you visualize your tasks and maintain focus.

Additionally, prioritize your tasks based on urgency. Note the tasks that require immediate attention first, followed by those that can be tackled later. This strategy will allow you to channel your energy towards important tasks and provide a sense of relief as you move on to subsequent tasks.

2. Divide Large Tasks into Smaller Components:

As an over-thinker, the sheer scope of tasks can feel daunting. However, splitting large tasks into smaller, more manageable parts can significantly improve your time management. For example, if your task is to complete an essay, start by creating an outline, then move on to research, drafting, and finally, proofreading.

Once you've subdivided your tasks, identify those needing immediate and undivided attention based on their deadline. Break down the task further according to a planned timeline. For instance, instead of merely stating "write draft," specify it to "write five pages of the draft by 1:30 pm." Directing your time and energy towards the foundational elements of the task can help identify potential hurdles, providing ample time to find solutions. This method can enhance motivation and allow you to monitor progress on an hourly basis.

3. Schedule Breaks between Tasks:

As an over-thinker, it's easy to become absorbed in your thoughts, neglecting your surroundings. This behavior can lead to exhaustion and burnout, reducing productivity. Hence, it's essential to take breaks between tasks to rejuvenate.

Taking regular breaks throughout the day enhances focus and productivity. Allowing your brain and body time to rest and recover enables you to return to your tasks with renewed energy and concentration. Short, frequent breaks have been shown to lead to higher productivity levels than working continuously without a break.

The Pomodoro technique, which involves working for 25 minutes followed by a 5-minute break, can be particularly effective. Some suggest taking a 30-minute break to stretch and move your body, which can clear your head. Try out different techniques to see which one works best for you.

Beyond boosting productivity, taking breaks offers numerous health benefits. Long periods of sitting can result in poor posture and back pain, and it can increase the risk of cardiovascular diseases. Breaks involving stretching, walking, or unwinding can mitigate such health risks, improving overall well-being.

4. Avoid Multitasking:

While multitasking may appear as an efficient way to handle multiple tasks, it's often a deceptive trap leading to ineffective results. Switching between tasks can elevate stress levels and reduce productivity, possibly leaving you with incomplete tasks at the end of the day. This is because multitasking splits your attention, causing minor details to be overlooked and lead to errors.

Concentrating solely on one task at a time is advisable to maximize productivity and efficiency. This doesn't imply devoting hours to a single task. Instead, it involves scheduling your time appropriately, setting achievable goals, and working based on your priorities. Minimizing distractions, such as silencing your phone or avoiding social media, can help maintain focus for extended periods.

After completing a smaller goal, you'll experience a sense of accomplishment, bringing you one step closer to your ultimate goal. Not only does this boost your self-confidence, but it also enables you to assess your progress and adjust as needed.

Quality always outweighs quantity. Instead of attempting to juggle multiple tasks at once, concentrate on one task at a time. This approach results in less stress, increased productivity, and, ultimately, superior outcomes.

5. Avoid Dwelling on Past Errors or Future Anxieties:

For over-thinkers, it's common to fall into a cycle of fretting over past mistakes or envisaging future uncertainties. However, this rumination can hamper productivity and overall well-being.

Here, time management becomes crucial. By focusing on the present moment, you can free yourself from the shackles of past regrets and anxieties. This shift in focus empowers you to take control of the present, effectively dealing with daily tasks without distractions.

This mindset can be fostered through mindfulness exercises. Mindfulness, the practice of staying in the present, has been shown to reduce stress levels, enhance cognitive functions, and boost creativity. When negative thoughts or worries do not weigh you down, you're better equipped to handle tasks and solve problems creatively.

Staying present can be challenging and requires deliberate effort. Techniques like breathing exercises, meditation, and journaling can help you maintain this mindset. By adopting a present-focused approach to time management, you can escape the cycle of overthinking and optimize your use of time and energy.

6. Prioritize Progress over Perfection:

Overthinking can be a significant obstacle to effective time management. Obsessing over countless details, striving for the "perfect" outcome, and procrastinating until the last minute can lead to inefficiency. However, it's crucial to understand that perfection is an unattainable standard, and chasing it will only result in frustration and overwhelm.

Instead, exercise patience with yourself. Understand that time management is a process, and progress is gradual. Celebrate small victories and view setbacks as opportunities to learn rather than failures.

Setting realistic goals is also crucial. Break down large tasks into smaller, manageable steps, and prioritize your to-do list based on importance. Remember, it's perfectly fine to seek help when needed, whether delegating tasks or seeking advice from a mentor or colleague.

Alongside patience and realistic goal setting, establish a routine or schedule. This can help you maintain focus, avoid distractions, and reduce time spent on decision-making.

7. Reward Yourself for Task Completion:

For over-thinkers, it's essential to continually find ways to stay motivated and on track. One effective strategy is rewarding yourself upon completing tasks, and this approach reinforces progress and encourages you to continue.

This strategy capitalizes on the brain's reward system, activated when we experience pleasurable feelings. Completing a task and rewarding yourself stimulates this system, creating a sense of satisfaction and accomplishment. This feeling can motivate you to tackle the next task.

Energy Management Tips

1. Recognize the Thoughts That Fuel Your Anxiety

As someone prone to overthinking, it's easy to become swamped with thoughts, leading to feelings of anxiety. To regain control, one effective energy management strategy is to identify the thoughts triggering your anxiety. This practice enables you to understand and address your anxiety's root causes.

Begin by distancing yourself slightly and observing your thought patterns. Pay attention to the thoughts that induce discomfort or unease. These may stem from future worries, past regrets, or even negative self-talk. After identifying these thoughts, keep a record and monitor when they surface.

By understanding your thought patterns, you can start to challenge them. Take some time to objectively evaluate these thoughts' validity. Are they fact-based or assumptive? Are they realistic or exaggerated? By questioning these thoughts, you can start reframing them in a more optimistic and realistic light.

2. Challenge Your Negative Thoughts: Are They Realistic or Beneficial?

As an over-thinker, it's easy to become entangled in negative thoughts, draining your mental energy. These thoughts may be rooted in fears, insecurities, or past experiences, often leading to feelings of anxiety, stress, or depression.

Challenging these negative thoughts can help you break free from the overthinking cycle and direct your energy toward more productive, positive thoughts. This process involves questioning whether these thoughts are realistic or beneficial.

Start by asking yourself whether the negative thought is based on facts or assumptions. Often, we are swayed by our biases or distorted thinking patterns, leading to irrational, unhelpful, or unrealistic thoughts.

After identifying the negative thought, question whether it serves you. Does it help you progress or hold you back? If the thought isn't beneficial, try to replace it with a more positive or realistic one.

3. Embrace Mindfulness and Concentrate on the Present Moment

Being prone to overthinking often means grappling with incessant thoughts, consuming significant mental energy. Practicing mindfulness and focusing on the present moment can help manage this energy effectively, reducing stress, anxiety, and even depressive symptoms.

Mindfulness involves consciously attending to the present moment without judgment or distractions from past or future concerns. You can practice mindfulness through meditation, focusing on your breath or body sensations, allowing you to let go of stress-inducing thoughts and anchor yourself in the present moment.

Moreover, you can incorporate mindfulness into your everyday life by fully engaging in each moment. For example, savor your food's taste, smell, and texture as you eat, or focus on the sounds and sights during a nature walk. These simple practices can help you stay grounded, reducing the energy drain caused by overthinking.

4. Engage in Regular Exercise to Alleviate Stress and Boost Mood

As an over-thinker, you may frequently feel engulfed in a whirlwind of stressful thoughts and anxiety, leaving you feeling drained and unmotivated. Regular exercise is a potent tool to combat stress and elevate your mood.

By participating in physical activity, your body releases endorphins, often known as "feel-good" hormones, which help combat stress and anxiety. Regular exercise can also enhance your energy levels by increasing your heart rate and blood flow, leading to an improved supply of oxygen and nutrients to your body.

Choose activities that you enjoy and fit into your lifestyle to get the most out of your exercise routine. Consistency is key, so make exercise a regular part of your routine.

5. Prioritize Quality Sleep, as Fatigue Can Exacerbate Anxiety

Switching off your mind at night and getting the rest you need can be challenging for an over-thinker. Adequate sleep is essential for managing anxiety and preventing it from escalating. Lack of sleep can worsen anxiety symptoms, making minor stressors seem insurmountable.

When you're sleep-deprived, your brain becomes more reactive to negative stimuli, and your ability to regulate emotions gets compromised. This means even minor stressors can trigger intense anxiety, leaving you feeling on edge and irritable.

On the other hand, sufficient sleep can enhance your ability to cope with stress and manage anxiety. Quality sleep allows your brain to process and integrate emotional experiences, helping you regulate your emotions and cope with anxiety triggers more effectively. Besides, sleep also positively impacts our physical health, reducing inflammation, improving immune function, and even enhancing our cognitive abilities.

Making sleep a priority might seem difficult, but it's essential for managing anxiety as an over-thinker. Improve your sleep quality by practicing good sleep hygiene, such as establishing a relaxing bedtime routine and avoiding electronics before bed. If you continue to struggle with sleep, consider consulting a healthcare provider for additional guidance and support.

6. Seek Social Support or Professional Help if Anxiety Severely Impacts Your Life

If you find yourself perpetually worried and anxious, taking steps to manage your energy and well-being is crucial. One of the most effective strategies is to talk to someone about your experiences. Keeping your worries to yourself only adds to their weight. By sharing them with a trusted friend, family member, or mental health professional, you can start to alleviate their burden.

Discussing your anxiety can help provide a new perspective and often offers valuable insights and advice from someone who may have had similar experiences. It also provides emotional support, helping you feel more grounded and better equipped to handle daily challenges.

If your anxiety is severe or adversely affects your quality of life, it may be necessary to seek professional help. This could involve consulting a therapist or counselor, who can provide guidance and support in managing your symptoms, or it may require medication to help alleviate anxiety symptoms.

In addition to seeking social support and professional help if necessary, various other energy management strategies can help over-thinkers feel more centered and focused. These strategies may include regular exercise, mindfulness practices, and engaging in creative or relaxing activities to reduce stress and anxiety. By adopting a proactive approach to managing your energy and well-being, you can start to feel more grounded, focused, and in control of your life.

7. Maintain a Balanced Diet for Optimal Mental Health

As an over-thinker, it's easy to overlook physical health while wrestling with a whirlwind of thoughts. However, maintaining a balanced diet can be vital in managing your energy and reducing anxiety. Certain foods can actually influence your mood, stress levels, and overall mental health.

Eating a diet rich in fruit, vegetables, lean proteins, whole grains, and healthy fats can positively impact your brain health. These foods provide essential nutrients that can enhance brain function, regulate mood, and reduce anxiety. For instance, foods rich in omega-3 fatty acids, like fish and flaxseeds, can reduce inflammation in the brain and improve mood. At the same time, complex carbohydrates in whole grains can help regulate serotonin levels. This hormone helps induce feelings of calm and well-being.

On the other hand, foods high in sugar, sodium, and unhealthy fats can lead to fluctuations in blood sugar, causing mood swings, irritability, and increased anxiety. Therefore, it's important to maintain a balanced diet and limit the intake of these foods.

Remember, maintaining a balanced diet is not just about what you eat but also when and how you eat. Try to maintain a regular eating schedule to prevent blood sugar fluctuations and manage your energy levels throughout the day. Also, avoid overeating or skipping meals, as it can lead to feelings of discomfort and anxiety.

Chapter 9: Daily Rituals for Long-Term Emotional Wellness

As an over-thinker and someone who has dealt with negative thoughts and emotions, you know that old habits die hard. Even after you've learned how to deal with these difficult emotions, it's challenging to implement your learned strategies and actually keep progressing steadily. Nowadays, it has become incredibly difficult to take time out for self-care and mental health. You often feel like you're just barely keeping your head above water and always rushing from one task to the next. It's unlikely that you even take a moment to breathe and be present in the moment. On top of this busy schedule, you must deal with negative emotions overwhelming you. You must learn to maintain your emotional wellness in the long term.

Your journey to reducing overthinking is like tending a garden.
https://unsplash.com/photos/1_vycvoMT6g?utm_source=unsplash&utm_medium=referral&utm_content=creditShareLink

Think of your journey as tending a garden. You've worked hard to plant the seeds, pull the weeds, and regularly water the plants. However, if you don't keep caring for your garden, it'll soon be overgrown and out of control. The same goes for your emotional wellbeing. Let's consider your journey, for example, where you've been struggling with overthinking thoughts and negative emotions, so you decide to take your life back and get in control of your emotions, which is a brave feat in and of itself. You read books, attend therapy sessions, and start practicing the techniques you've learned. Over time, you'll begin to feel like you've got a better handle on managing your emotions and thought patterns.

As time passes, you may get busy with friends, family, your career, or other responsibilities and completely forego your emotional wellness. You might skip therapy sessions or stop your daily mindfulness exercises. Even though you'll feel in control for a while, before you know it, you'll start slipping back into your old negative patterns and start feeling overwhelmed again. At this point, you'll realize that while you had learned and practiced techniques for managing your negative thoughts, you did not try to maintain them. You eventually relapsed back into your unhealthy emotional habits. So, why not be proactive and not let things get so out of hand in the first place? You've already gone through different techniques and exercises to manage overthinking and negative thoughts. Go one step further and incorporate some daily micro-rituals that ensure you stay on a healthy emotional path.

Micro-rituals will help you create a foundation of emotional well-being that will stay intact even when life becomes busy and stressful. Understandably, you wouldn't want to think about managing your emotions your whole life. You should then develop healthy habits that make it so you don't have to. Incorporating healthy micro-habits into your routine will help you manage your emotions and build resilience and emotional strength that will carry you through tough times. Think of it like building a house. You can have the best quality construction materials and techniques, but if you do not lay out and maintain a strong foundation, the structure is doomed to collapse. The same goes for your emotional foundations.

That's where this bonus chapter comes in. It will include some helpful techniques that don't take up a lot of your time and are easy to incorporate into your routine. Think of these rituals as mini self-care practices. Doing them is equivalent to giving yourself a tiny boost of happiness and positivity daily.

Breathwork

Breathwork might sound like some new-age hippie trend. However, it's anything but that. At its core, breathwork is simply the practice of intentionally controlling your breath to achieve certain outcomes. It is a powerful tool for putting a stop to your patterns of rumination and self-doubt. It might sound too good to be true, but the benefits of breathwork are scientifically proven. Breathing deeply and slowly signals your brain to activate the parasympathetic nervous system. This part of your nervous system is responsible for "rest and digest" activities like slowing your heart rate and reducing muscle tension.

Its benefits go beyond just feeling relaxed. Regular breathwork practice has been shown to improve immune function, lower blood pressure, and increase the overall sense of well-being. When limiting overthinking and negative thinking, breathwork can be a powerful tool.

So how do you actually do breathwork? There are a variety of techniques out there, but a few of the most popular include box breathing, pranayama, and 4-7-8 breathing.

- Box breathing is a simple technique that involves inhaling for a count of four, holding the breath for a count of four, exhaling for a count of four, and holding it again for a count of four. Repeat this cycle for a few minutes, focusing on the sensation of your breath moving in and out.

- Pranayama is a more advanced technique that involves manipulating the breath in different ways to achieve specific effects. One example is alternate nostril breathing, which involves blocking one nostril with your thumb, inhaling through the other, then blocking that nostril with your ring finger and exhaling through the first. Repeat for several rounds, focusing on the sensation of the breath moving through your nostrils.

- The 4-7-8 breathing is a technique that involves inhaling deeply through your nose for a count of four, holding it for a count of seven, then exhaling through your mouth for a count of eight. Repeat for several rounds, focusing on the sensation of your breath moving in and out.

The key to any breath-work practice is to start small and work your way up. Even a few minutes daily can greatly impact your overall well-being.

Gratitude

When life gets tough, getting caught up in negative thoughts and emotions can be easy. That's why practicing gratitude can be such a powerful tool in managing overthinking and negative thinking patterns. By focusing on what you're grateful for, you can shift your attention away from what you lack and towards what you already have. A regular gratitude practice can increase positive emotions such as joy, contentment, and optimism. When you focus on the good things in your life, you will become more aware of the positive experiences happening around you. At the same time, practicing gratitude can decrease negative emotions like envy, resentment, and regret. There are so many different ways to practice gratitude, and what works for one person may not work for another. Here are a few techniques to help you get started:

- **Keep a gratitude journal:** Each day, write down a few things you are grateful for. These could be big things, like landing your dream job, or small things, like a beautiful sunset or a warm cup of coffee. The act of writing down what you are grateful for can help you cultivate a more positive mindset and increase feelings of happiness and well-being.

- **Make a gratitude list:** If you don't have time to write in a journal every day, try making a gratitude list instead. Sit down for a few minutes and write down everything you are grateful for. You may be surprised by how long your list becomes! You can keep your gratitude list somewhere visible, like on your fridge or next to your bed, as a reminder of all the good things in your life.

- **Express gratitude to others:** Another way to practice gratitude is by expressing it directly to others. Say *thank you* to a friend or family member who has been there for you, or write a note of appreciation to someone who has made a difference in your life.

- **Write a gratitude letter:** Choose someone who has positively impacted your life and write them a letter expressing your gratitude. Be specific about the things they have done for you and how it has made a difference. You can either send the letter or read it to them in person.

No matter how you express gratitude, it is important to make it a regular practice. Try setting aside a few minutes each day to focus on what you are grateful for. Over time, you will find that this simple practice has a powerful impact on your mental health and overall well-being.

Contemplative Reading

When it comes to managing overthinking and negative thoughts, people often focus on taking action or talking to others for support. But what about the power of quiet contemplation through reading? Contemplative reading differs from regular reading because it requires you to slow down and engage with the text. It's about reading for self-discovery, not just for entertainment. This means taking the time to reflect on what you're reading, asking yourself questions, and making connections to your own life experiences.

So, what types of books are good for contemplative reading? Anything that allows for introspection and self-reflection can be useful. Self-help books, spiritual texts, and poetry are all great options. It's not about the genre of the book but rather the mindset you bring to the reading experience. Here are some great books you can start with:

- The Untethered Soul by Michael A. Singer
- The Power of Now by Eckhart Tolle
- Wherever You Go, There You Are by Jon Kabat-Zinn
- The Book of Awakening by Mark Nepo
- The Tao of Pooh by Benjamin Hoff
- The Alchemist by Paulo Coelho
- The Four Agreements by Don Miguel Ruiz
- A New Earth by Eckhart Tolle
- The Art of Happiness by Dalai Lama XIV and Howard C. Cutler.

Take the time to reflect on what you're reading, ask yourself questions, and connect to your life experiences. Set aside 10-15 minutes each day to read a few pages with intention, and over time, you'll start to notice a difference in your ability to regulate your emotions and respond to challenging situations.

Social Media Detox

Do you ever feel like social media is sucking the life out of you? A constant stream of updates, likes, comments, and notifications leave you feeling drained and disconnected. It can be even worse for over-thinkers and negative thinkers – a breeding ground for comparison, self-doubt, and FOMO. Think about it – how many times have you mindlessly scrolled through your feed only to feel more stressed or anxious? How often do you compare yourself to others online and end up feeling inadequate? Social media can be a powerful tool, but it can also be toxic if you're not careful.

By doing a social media detox, you give yourself the space and freedom to focus on your own life and thoughts without the constant noise and distractions. Even if you can't completely disconnect from it, reducing the time you spend on it can make a world of difference. When was the last time you took a break from social media and just lived in the moment without feeling the need to document every experience or check your notifications?

Start by setting boundaries for yourself, like limiting your social media use to a certain amount of time each day. When you do indulge, try to follow accounts that uplift and inspire you instead of ones that bring you down. If you're feeling up for it, go for a social media detox altogether. Give yourself the gift of a few days, or even a week, without the pressure to keep up with everyone else's highlight reel. Take that time to reconnect with yourself and rediscover what truly brings you joy.

Moving Your Body

Imagine waking up to a beautiful morning, and instead of immediately reaching for your phone to scroll through social media or emails, you slip into your workout clothes and step outside for a refreshing jog. As you move your body, you start to feel a sense of lightness and clarity of mind. You notice the sun shining, the birds chirping, and the fresh air filling your lungs. It's a reminder that you are alive and well.

Physical exercise, whether it's jogging, yoga, dancing, or weightlifting, has numerous benefits for emotional wellness. It releases endorphins, the "feel-good" chemicals in your brain, and reduces stress and anxiety, improves sleep, and boosts self-confidence. Incorporating physical activity into your daily routine can help you maintain a healthy mind-body connection and prevent overthinking and negative thoughts from taking over.

Start small by committing to just 10-15 minutes of physical activity each day and gradually build up to longer sessions. You can also find ways to incorporate movement into your daily routine, such as taking the stairs instead of the elevator or doing some stretching while watching TV. Whatever form of physical exercise you choose, make it enjoyable and sustainable for you, and notice how it positively impacts your overall well-being.

Happy Smoothie

For many people, mornings are synonymous with grogginess and sluggishness but fear not! There is a simple, delicious solution to start your day on the right foot; a happy smoothie.

Creating a happy smoothie can be a fun and easy mini-ritual to add to your morning routine. It doesn't have to be complicated or time-consuming. In fact, you can whip up a delicious and nutritious happy smoothie in just a few minutes. Why a happy smoothie, you ask? Besides being tasty, a happy smoothie can improve your emotional wellness by providing essential nutrients and stabilizing your blood sugar levels. It's a great way to start your day on a positive note and can even keep negative thoughts at bay.

Here are some delicious happy smoothie recipes to try out:

- **Berry Bliss** - Blend together strawberries, blueberries, bananas, Greek yogurt, almond milk, and a drizzle of honey for a delicious and refreshing start to your day.

- **Green Goodness** - Combine spinach, kale, avocado, banana, almond milk, and a dash of cinnamon for a nutritious and energizing smoothie.

- **Tropical Paradise** - Mix pineapple, mango, coconut milk, banana, and a scoop of protein powder for a taste of the tropics in a glass.

Incorporating a happy smoothie into your morning routine can be a small but powerful step toward improving your overall well-being and reducing negative thinking patterns.

Mojo Bag or Comfort Pouch

As you go about your day, you may feel like you're carrying a heavy load on your shoulders. Negative thoughts, stress, and anxiety can weigh you down and leave you feeling drained. What if you could carry a little piece of comfort with you everywhere you go? A comfort pouch is a small bag filled with items that bring you joy and comfort. It's like a portable happy place that you can turn to when you need a little pick-me-up. The best part? You can customize it to suit your needs.

To create your comfort pouch, choose a small bag you love. It can be a pouch, a drawstring bag, or even a pocket-sized purse. Next, think about the items that bring you comfort. It could be a piece of your favorite candy, a small plush toy, a photo of a loved one, or even a mini journal to write down your thoughts. Some items you might consider including in your comfort kit:

- A favorite scented candle or essential oil
- A cozy blanket or shawl
- A small stuffed animal or figurine that makes you smile
- A handwritten note with a positive affirmation or quote
- A favorite book or magazine
- A stress ball or fidget toy
- A favorite tea or hot cocoa mix
- A small photo album or scrapbook of happy memories

As you collect items for your comfort pouch, consider how they make you feel. Do they bring back happy memories? Do they make you feel safe and loved? Now that you have your comfort pouch, you can turn to it whenever you need a little boost. Feeling anxious before a big meeting? Take a deep breath and reach for your favorite candy. Feeling overwhelmed by your to-do list? Take a quick break and look at your photo of a loved one. Instead of letting negative thoughts and feelings drag you down, you will have a physical reminder of the things that bring you joy and comfort.

Group Sports

Do you often find yourself stuck in your own thoughts, overanalyzing everything, and feeling overwhelmed? Participating in group sports can be a great way to break out of that cycle and improve your emotional wellness. Group sports allow you to disconnect from your thoughts and provide a sense of community and belonging that can help combat feelings of isolation and loneliness. Whether it's a casual game of basketball with friends or a yoga class with strangers, participating in group sports can help you feel more connected to others and the world around you. Here are a few group sports to consider:

- **Basketball:** Lace up your sneakers and head to the nearest court for a pickup game or join a local league for some friendly competition. The fast-paced nature of basketball can help you focus on the game and leave your overthinking tendencies behind.

- **Yoga:** If you're looking for a more meditative approach to group sports, consider joining a yoga class. The calming atmosphere and guidance of an instructor can also help you quieten your mind and let go of negative thought patterns.

- **Soccer:** Get your kicks on the field and join a recreational league in your area. Soccer is a great way to challenge yourself physically and mentally, as it requires strategic thinking and teamwork.

- **Kickboxing:** A high-intensity workout that combines martial arts and cardio, kickboxing classes can be a great way to release stress and aggression in a safe and controlled environment. Many gyms and fitness studios offer group kickboxing classes.

Overcoming Resistance to Daily Rituals

The struggle to create new habits is all too common. You read about a new micro-ritual promising to improve your life, and you're pumped to try it. But then life gets in the way, and before you know it, you've given up on the ritual altogether. It's frustrating, but it doesn't have to be that way. When you start, you will probably find yourself hitting snooze on your morning alarm instead of jumping out of bed and into your daily micro-rituals. It'll be a while before you can establish healthy habits that stick.

One of the biggest barriers to establishing daily rituals is resistance. It's easy to succumb to the temptation to skip your morning meditation or evening walk, but don't worry; *you're not alone*. The good news is that with a few simple strategies, you can overcome resistance and make daily rituals a consistent part of your routine. First, start small. Don't overwhelm yourself with lofty goals that are impossible to achieve. Instead, start with one small habit and gradually build from there. For example, commit to doing just five minutes of stretching each morning or drinking a glass of water as soon as you wake up. Many people make the mistake of trying to implement too many changes at once, which can quickly become overwhelming and lead to giving up altogether.

Instead, focus on starting with one small change at a time. For example, if you want to start a daily gratitude journal, begin by committing to writing just one thing you're grateful for each day. By starting small, you're setting yourself up for success and building momentum toward bigger changes. As you get used to your new micro-ritual, you can gradually increase the frequency or duration to make it more meaningful. Remember, small changes can lead to big results.

Do you ever notice how the little things you do every day can greatly impact your emotional wellness? It's easy to get bogged down in the busyness of life and forget to take care of yourself. As an overthinker, breaking the cycle of negative thought patterns and finding emotional balance can be difficult. However, incorporating micro-rituals into your daily routine can shift your mindset and improve your overall well-being.

Conclusion

Many people are plagued with overthinking and its effect on their mental well-being. Overthinking and chronic anxiety have been shown to activate the body's stress response, which causes physical symptoms like (increased cardiac activity and high blood pressure) and cognitive symptoms (such as difficulty recalling things and focusing).

Fear and worry can significantly impact your physical health and lead to diabetes, coronary heart disease, and even cancer. This brings us to the important question: Will you continue to let these negative emotions and overthinking patterns determine the direction of your life?

The time to stop overanalyzing things and take control of your thoughts is right now. You have the power to dominate your thoughts, eliminate negative ideologies, and control your feelings with the right approaches and strategies.

By now, you should have a thorough understanding of the psychology behind overthinking and its negative impact on your life. In this book, you will also find a few practical strategies that you can implement to help you recognize your overthinking tendencies and overcome them.

This book has also emphasized the importance of self-care and self-compassion. To live a fulfilling life, you must prioritize your physical, emotional, and mental well-being. You can achieve this by taking time for yourself each day.

Acknowledge that your journey toward emotional wellness is going to be a rough one. You will need to practice self-compassion and patience as you work towards creating a more fulfilling life for yourself. Although the strategies outlined in this book aren't exactly quick fixes, they are sure to help you improve your emotional and mental well-being in the long run.

Among others, a vital lesson in this book is mindfulness and living in the moment. When you live in the moment, you will worry much less about the future. Incorporating mindfulness and breathing exercises into your daily life can help you stay grounded and remain in the present.

Another thing you need to take away from this book is the power of positive thinking. Reframing negative thoughts and focusing on any situation's positive aspects can easily shift your mindset and improve your mood. Don't forget to celebrate the little victories you enjoy and practice self-compassion all the way.

Finally, remember that seeking help doesn't mean you're weak. Instead, it is actually proof of your great strength. Don't hesitate to seek professional help or join a support group when you're struggling with overthinking and negative thought patterns. It can be an invaluable tool on your journey toward emotional wellness.

Here's another book by Andy Gardner that you might like

Free Bonus from Andy Gardner

Hi!

My name is Andy Gardner, and first off, I want to THANK YOU for reading my book.

Now you have a chance to join my exclusive email list related to human psychology and self-development so you can get the ebook below for free as well as the potential to get more ebooks for free! Simply click the link below to join.

P.S. Remember that it's 100% free to join the list.

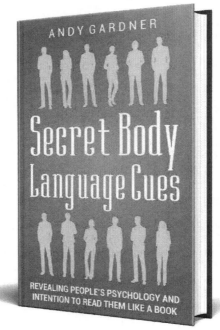

Access your free bonuses here:
https://livetolearn.lpages.co/andy-gardner-stop-overthinking-paperback/

References

Self-reflection: Definition and how to do it. (n.d.). The Berkeley Well-Being Institute. https://www.berkeleywellbeing.com/what-is-self-reflection.html

(N.d.). Apa.org. https://www.apa.org/ptsd-guideline/patients-and-families/cognitive-behavioral#:~:text=Cognitive%20behavioral%20therapy%20(CBT)%20is,disorders%2C%20and%20severe%20mental%20illness.

(N.d.). Usnews.com. https://health.usnews.com/wellness/mind/how-to-improve-time-management

(N.d.). Yogabasics.com. https://www.yogabasics.com/connect/yoga-blog/mindful-journal-prompts/

20 most common time management problems + tips. (n.d.). Time. https://www.actitime.com/time-management-guide/time-management-problems-and-solutions

4 ways to stop negative thinking. (n.d.). Mcleanhospital.org. https://www.mcleanhospital.org/essential/negative-thinking

5 tips for changing negative self beliefs. (2014, October 30). Psych Central. https://psychcentral.com/blog/5-tips-for-changing-negative-self-beliefs

Abpp, M. S. P., & Sally Winston, P. (2018, April 26). Unwanted intrusive thoughts. Adaa.org. https://adaa.org/learn-from-us/from-the-experts/blog-posts/consumer/unwanted-intrusive-thoughts

AbuHasan, Q., Reddy, V., & Siddiqui, W. (2022). Neuroanatomy, Amygdala. StatPearls Publishing.

Ali. (2022, April 14). 5 real ways to understand yourself better (and be self-aware). Tracking Happiness. https://www.trackinghappiness.com/how-to-understand-yourself/

Are you an overthinker? (n.d.-a). Psychology Today. https://www.psychologytoday.com/intl/blog/the-runaway-mind/202001/are-you-overthinker

Are you an overthinker? (n.d.-b). Psychology Today. https://www.psychologytoday.com/us/blog/the-runaway-mind/202001/are-you-overthinker

Banerjee, S. (2022). Mindful Breathing: An introduction to mindful and relaxing breathing. S. Banerjee.

Bertin, M. (2023, March 28). A guided walking meditation for daily life. Mindful; Mindful Communications & Such PBC. https://www.mindful.org/daily-mindful-walking-practice/

Borchard, T. (2016, February 19). 5 ways to free yourself from dark and obsessive thoughts. Everydayhealth.com; Everyday Health. https://www.everydayhealth.com/columns/therese-borchard-sanity-break/ways-free-yourself-from-dark-obsessive-thoughts/

Bradshaw, F. (2021, July 7). How to turn negative thoughts into positive actions. Mind Tools. https://www.mindtools.com/blog/how-to-turn-negative-thoughts-into-positive-actions/

Cherry, K. (2011, May 18). How brain neurons change over time from life experience. Verywell Mind. https://www.verywellmind.com/what-is-brain-plasticity-2794886

Cho, H., Ryu, S., Noh, J., & Lee, J. (2016). The effectiveness of daily mindful breathing practices on test anxiety of students. PloS One, 11(10), e0164822. https://doi.org/10.1371/journal.pone.0164822

Climan, A., RDN, & CD-N. (2023, January 11). Cognitive reframing. Drugwatch.com; Drugwatch. https://www.drugwatch.com/mental-health/therapy/cognitive-restructuring/

Coaches, M. T. (2022, May 20). 8 ways on how to stop overthinking everything. Tonyrobbins.com. https://www.tonyrobbins.com/mental-health/how-to-stop-overthinking/

Correia, K. (2022, May 31). Six everyday rituals for mental health. Wanderlust. https://wanderlust.com/journal/6-everyday-rituals-for-mental-health/

David, S. (2016, November 10). 3 ways to better understand your emotions. Harvard Business Review. https://hbr.org/2016/11/3-ways-to-better-understand-your-emotions

Devroux, T. (2020, March 26). Learn by doing nothing: Emotions & thoughts in meditation. Mindworks Meditation. https://mindworks.org/blog/learn-by-doing-nothing-emotions-and-thoughts-in-meditation/

DiGiulio, S., Millard, E., Migala, J., & Young, A. (n.d.). Self-care: How to do it right now. Everydayhealth.com. https://www.everydayhealth.com/wellness/top-self-care-tips-for-being-stuck-at-home-during-the-coronavirus-pandemic/

Do, A. (2022, December 25). Why it's more important to manage your energy than your time. Any.Do Blog | Productivity Tips & Trends, Delivered; Any.do. https://www.any.do/blog/why-its-more-important-to-manage-your-energy-than-your-time/

Entona, K. (2021, February 17). Daily wellness rituals to add to your routine. Country Life Vitamins; Country Life. https://www.countrylifevitamins.com/blog/everyday/daily-wellness-rituals/

GoodRx - error. (n.d.). Goodrx.com. https://www.goodrx.com/health-topic/mental-health/how-can-i-stop-overthinking-everything

Hartney, E., & MSc, M. A. (2011, March 3). 10 cognitive distortions that can cause negative thinking. Verywell Mind. https://www.verywellmind.com/ten-cognitive-distortions-identified-in-cbt-22412

Hill, J. T. (2019, December 11). What is self-worth and how to recognize yours. Lifehack. https://www.lifehack.org/854916/what-is-self-worth

How do you measure your self-worth? (n.d.). Psychology Today. https://www.psychologytoday.com/intl/blog/what-mentally-strong-people-dont-do/201707/how-do-you-measure-your-self-worth

Hubbling, A., Reilly-Spong, M., Kreitzer, M. J., & Gross, C. R. (2014). How mindfulness changed my sleep: focus groups with chronic insomnia patients. BMC Complementary and Alternative Medicine, 14(1), 50. https://doi.org/10.1186/1472-6882-14-50

Intermountain Healthcare. (2020, November 4). What's the difference between worry and anxiety? Intermountainhealthcare.org. https://intermountainhealthcare.org/blogs/topics/live-well/2020/11/whats-the-difference-between-worry-and-anxiety/

Jabarin, S. A., Lofgren, E. A., & Sakumoto, S. (2005). Aging and environmental stress cracking of PET, its copolymers and blends: Sections 3.2-3.3. In Handbook of Thermoplastic Polyesters (pp. 1051–1071). Wiley-VCH Verlag GmbH & Co. KGaA.

Kabat-Zinn, J. (2019, March 20). A meditation on observing thoughts, non-judgmentally. Mindful; Mindful Communications & Such PBC. https://www.mindful.org/a-meditation-on-observing-thoughts-non-judgmentally/

Kaiser, B. N., Haroz, E. E., Kohrt, B. A., Bolton, P. A., Bass, J. K., & Hinton, D. E. (2015). "Thinking too much": A systematic review of a common idiom of distress. Social Science & Medicine (1982), 147, 170–183. https://doi.org/10.1016/j.socscimed.2015.10.044

LaCaille, L., Patino-Fernandez, A. M., Monaco, J., Ding, D., Upchurch Sweeney, C. R., Butler, C. D., Soskolne, C. L., Gidron, Y., Gidron, Y., Turner, J. R., Turner, J. R., Butler, J., Burns, M. N., Mohr, D. C., Molton, I., Carroll, D., Critchley, H., Nagai, Y., Baumann, L. C., ... Söderback, I. (2013). Expressive Writing and Health. In Encyclopedia of Behavioral Medicine (pp. 735–741). Springer New York.

Lamothe, C. (2019, November 15). How to stop overthinking: 14 strategies. Healthline. https://www.healthline.com/health/how-to-stop-overthinking

Martin, L. (2021, February 18). 10 rock-solid time management strategies to boost your productivity. Time Doctor Blog; Time Doctor. https://www.timedoctor.com/blog/time-management-strategies/

McCallum, K. (n.d.). When overthinking becomes a problem & what you can do about it. Houstonmethodist.org. https://www.houstonmethodist.org/blog/articles/2021/apr/when-overthinking-becomes-a-problem-and-what-you-can-do-about-it/

Murrihy, C. (2021, September 9). The 3 main types of overthinking and how to overcome them. Childline. https://www.childline.ie/the-3-main-types-of-overthinking-and-how-to-overcome-them/

No title. (n.d.). Study.com. https://study.com/learn/lesson/stress-management-overview-benefits.html

Oppong, T. (2019, July 25). Stress is a byproduct of overthinking. Ladders. https://www.theladders.com/career-advice/stress-is-a-byproduct-of-overthinking

Our, L. A. (2020, September 9). How to Stop Overthinking. Verywell Mind. https://www.verywellmind.com/how-to-know-when-youre-overthinking-5077069

Overthinking: Definition, causes, & how to stop. (n.d.). The Berkeley Well-Being Institute. https://www.berkeleywellbeing.com/overthinking.html

Overview - Generalised anxiety disorder in adults. (n.d.). Nhs.uk. https://www.nhs.uk/mental-health/conditions/generalised-anxiety-disorder/overview/

Present, P. R. (2021, February 2). The psychology behind chronic overthinking – and how to get rid of this toxic habit. International Business Times. https://www.ibtimes.com/psychology-behind-chronic-overthinking-how-get-rid-toxic-habit-3136038

Randles, D., Flett, G. L., Nash, K. A., McGregor, I. D., & Hewitt, P. L. (2010). Dimensions of perfectionism, behavioral inhibition, and rumination. Personality and Individual Differences, 49(2), 83–87. https://doi.org/10.1016/j.paid.2010.03.002

Rao, G. (2016, September 13). What are negative thoughts? Yourdost.com. https://yourdost.com/blog/2016/09/what-are-negative-thoughts.html?q=/blog/2016/09/what-are-negative-thoughts.html&

Raypole, C. (2019, March 15). Physical symptoms of anxiety: What does it feel like? Healthline. https://www.healthline.com/health/physical-symptoms-of-anxiety

Rebecca Joy Stanborough, M. F. A. (2020, February 4). Cognitive restructuring: Techniques and examples. Healthline. https://www.healthline.com/health/cognitive-restructuring

Rinpoche, G. (2018, September 27). 20 journaling prompts for working with emotions — life transition coach. Life Transition Coach | Mental + Emotional Wellness Coaching | Yoga Nidra + Meditation Guidance. https://www.kimroberts.co/blog/20-journaling-prompts-for-working-with-emotions

Robinson, L., & Melinda Smith, M. A. (n.d.). Stress management - Helpguide.org. https://www.helpguide.org/articles/stress/stress-management.htm

Santilli, M. (2023, March 10). How to stop overthinking: Causes and ways to cope. Forbes. https://www.forbes.com/health/mind/what-causes-overthinking-and-6-ways-to-stop/

Schimelpfening, N. (2011, January 26). What is mindfulness-based cognitive therapy (MBCT)? Verywell Mind. https://www.verywellmind.com/mindfulness-based-cognitive-therapy-1067396

Sharma, S. (2021, July 20). Cognitive reframing: Definition, benefits & how cognitive reframing helps in stress management. Calm Sage. https://www.calmsage.com/what-is-cognitive-reframing/

Teut, M., Roesner, E. J., Ortiz, M., Reese, F., Binting, S., Roll, S., Fischer, H. F., Michalsen, A., Willich, S. N., & Brinkhaus, B. (2013). Mindful walking in psychologically distressed individuals: a randomized controlled trial. Evidence-Based Complementary and Alternative Medicine: ECAM, 2013, 489856. https://doi.org/10.1155/2013/489856

The Counseling Teacher. (2018, March 19). 5 ways to reframe negative thoughts. Confident Counselors. https://confidentcounselors.com/2018/03/19/reframe-negative-thoughts/

Therapeutic ways to alter negative thoughts. (n.d.). WebMD. https://www.webmd.com/depression/features/therapy-change-negative-thoughts

Tigar, L. (2021, January 20). 20 micro (yet mighty) self-care challenges that make any day better. Real Simple. https://www.realsimple.com/work-life/life-strategies/inspiration-motivation/small-self-care-challenges

Vorkapic, C., Leal, S., Alves, H., Douglas, M., Britto, A., & Dantas, E. H. M. (2021). Born to move: a review on the impact of physical exercise on brain health and the evidence from human controlled trials. Arquivos de Neuro-Psiquiatria, 79(6), 536–550. https://pubmed.ncbi.nlm.nih.gov/34320058/

Walinga, J. (2014). 16.2 stress and coping. In Introduction to Psychology - 1st Canadian Edition. BCcampus.

What are intrusive thoughts? (n.d.). WebMD. https://www.webmd.com/mental-health/intrusive-thoughts

What is cognitive reframing and why do therapists use it? (n.d.). Betterhelp.com. https://www.betterhelp.com/advice/therapy/what-is-cognitive-reframing-and-why-do-therapists-use-it/

What Is Worry? (2023, February 21). Psychology Tools. https://www.psychologytools.com/resource/what-is-worry/

Why worrying is unhelpful, and one thing you can do instead. (n.d.). Psychology Today. https://www.psychologytoday.com/us/blog/the-mindful-self-express/201903/why-worrying-is-unhelpful-and-one-thing-you-can-do-instead

Wignall, N. (2021, February 17). 7 psychological reasons you overthink everything. Nick Wignall. https://nickwignall.com/7-psychological-reasons-you-overthink-everything/

Wooll, M. (n.d.). 20 stress management techniques: Your guide to stress-management. Betterup.com. https://www.betterup.com/blog/stress-management-techniques

Printed in Great Britain
by Amazon

28306613R00066